Rending
the Curtain

The Cross as Completion of the
Old Testament Day of Atonement
(second edition)

an eight-week study of Scripture

Tammy L. Priest
2018

Rending the Curtain: The Cross as Completion of the Old Testament Day of Atonement, second edition
© 2018 Tammy L. Priest
Beginning With Moses
www.beginningwithmoses.com

Digital cover art © Tammy Priest, Rending the Curtain
Back cover photo credit: Alysia H. Grimes
Feast Icons (Appendix A) © Tammy L. Priest
ISBN: 978-0-9822526-7-3

Scripture Translations
All Scripture references are from the New International Version (NIV), unless otherwise specified.

BECK .... The Holy Bible In the Language of Today by William F. Beck (Copyright © 1976 Leader Publishing Company, New Haven, Missouri)

DRV .... Douay-Rheims Version (public domain)

HCSB ..... Holman Christian Standard Bible (Copyright © 1999, 2000, 2002, 2003 by Holman Bible Publishers, Nashville, Tennessee)

JPS .... Jewish Publication Society (Copyright © 1917, The Jewish Publication Society of America)

KJV......... King James Version (public domain)

NAS........ New American Standard Bible (Copyright © 1960, 1962, 1968, 1 971, 1972, 1973, 1975, 1977, 1995 by The Lockman Foundation, La Habra, California)

NIV .... New International Version (Copyright © 1973, 1978, 1984 by Biblica)

NKJ .... New King James Version (Copyright © 1982 by Thomas Nelson, Inc.)

RSV .... Revised Standard Version (Copyright © 1946, 1952, and 1971, the Division of Christian Education of the National Council of the Churches of Christ in the United States of America)

Contents

Introduction

Apples & Honey

"This is to be a lasting ordinance for you...because on this day atonement will be made for you, to cleanse you."
Leviticus 16:29-30

Some of my sweetest childhood memories are of gathering downstairs in the synagogue, feasting on apples drenched in honey. We were celebrating *Rosh Hashanah*, the Jewish New Year. This apples and honey tradition, which follows the worship service, is meant to celebrate the year behind and usher in a sweet year to come. You see, honey is symbolic of God's Promised Land, which He said would be flowing with milk and honey.[1] It also reminds us of God's sustenance to the Israelites during their journey to that Promised Land, for Moses said the manna from heaven tasted like honey wafers.[2]

And so, as the congregation partakes of this sweet snack, we are reminded of God's sustenance in years past, and we look forward to a new year of sweet fellowship in the promised land of His Presence. The congregation prays together, *May it be Thy will, O Lord our God and God of our Fathers, that you renew us for a good and sweet year.*

On the eve of such rejoicing, however, there is also the anticipation of mourning. Because, as the sun sets on *Rosh Hashanah*, all eyes and hearts look forward to *Yom Kippur*, the Jewish Day of Atonement, just ten days ahead. For a Jew, simply hearing the words "*Yom Kippur*" ushers in a solemnity, a seriousness unlike any other. Non-Jews may know that *Yom Kippur* is a Jewish holy day, or even that it is observed by fasting from food and all activities except worship. But what exactly is it?

In a nutshell, *Yom Kippur* is the annual ritual through which spiritual atonement is purchased for the nation of Israel. Its provision is found in Leviticus 16. But what does this ancient Hebrew holy day have to do with the Cross of Christianity? In a word: everything.

The God-ordained purpose of *Yom Kippur* was to purchase atonement and reconciliation for God's people so that He might continue to dwell with them. At the heart of the *Yom Kippur* ritual, according to God's command, was the sacrifice of a perfect lamb's blood in His own Presence, inside the Holy of Holies. Fifteen hundred years later, Christianity was born. At its heart is the same message of forgiveness and reconciliation between God and man. And the source of this forgiveness is the blood of *the* Lamb—God's only, perfect Son.

The purpose and effect of *Yom Kippur* and the Cross are one in the same. Yet rather than existing as similar atonement rites of two different faiths, *Yom Kippur* and the Cross mark the point at which the two faiths converge. In fact, at the center of this union, we can discover that Judaism and Christianity are not separate faiths at all. Instead, we see that one is the perfect confirmation, fulfillment and continuation of the other.

While the observance of *Yom Kippur* today looks very different from the Levitical commands (see Appendix C), a study of the original Biblical ritual can bring great meaning to people of faith. And so, in the pages to come, we will examine God's Word from the book of Leviticus, discovering the ritual's divine details as He originally and perfectly instructed. We will look at the role of the five key "players" in this drama: God Almighty, His Tabernacle, the High Priest, the sacrificial lambs, and the people for whom atonement was purchased.

If you are a Christian, I hope this study will bring new meaning to the Cross, and a greater understanding of why there really was no other way for the Savior to save us. I hope you will learn that when Jesus said He had come to fulfill the law,[3] He meant more than "just" the fact that He would live a life of spiritual perfection. Jesus also meant that He had come to shed His own blood in order to fulfill God's existing Law of Atonement for the nation of humanity.

If you happen to be Jewish, I hope these pages give you an understanding of how the Torah and the New Testament of Christianity connect. How they logically flow into one another instead of diverging at the birth of Christ. And how people like me can therefore say with full assurance that we are, indeed, still Jewish. Not in spite of our belief in Jesus but because of it.

Whatever your background, it is my prayer that this intersection between *Yom Kippur* and the Cross will enlighten you. And I pray that we will all be awed and inspired by our Holy God's determination to draw close to an unholy people.

Don't Turn the Page!

Before embarking on this journey, let us consider first *t'shuva*.
Literally "turning," *t'shuva* is the process of self-examination and turning
back to God that takes place during the ten days between *Rosh Hashanah*
and *Yom Kippur*. It is a very
sobering time, because
during these days we are to
ask each other—*in person*—
for forgiveness of hurts or

> "If therefore you are presenting your
> offering at the altar, and there remember
> that your brother has something against
> you, leave your offering there before the
> altar, and go your way; first be reconciled
> to your brother, and then come and
> present your offering.
> Matthew 5:23-24

offenses committed during the year. Reconciled to the people around us,
on *Yom Kippur* each person is then able to focus solely on sins committed
against God alone.

**As we together draw closer to the most sacred place in
Scripture—the Holy of Holies, consider whether there is anyone to
whom you need to be reconciled, no matter where the blame lies,**

> As far as it depends on
> you, live at peace with
> everyone.
> Romans 12:18

before you approach God's altar.

Week One

Setting the Stage

Yom Kippur is the only day each year that the Lord allowed anyone

to enter the Holy of Holies. Here, in the innermost chamber of the

Tabernacle—and later the Temple—is where God's tangible Presence

resided. But "allowed" isn't really the right word. The Lord didn't just

permit the High Priest to enter His Presence, He *demanded* it. What would

happen on this day was so sacred, so important, that it must be done in

the very Presence of the Almighty God.

In order for us to even begin to grasp the significance of the

annual atonement ritual, it is best to understand some key background

information about the Jewish Day of Atonement. For this basic

understanding, we will look at five simple things: (1) what the words

Yom Kippur mean; (2) the significance of when the ritual takes place; (3)

our personal need for atonement; (4) the Old Testament sacrificial system; and (5) the magnitude of the date God assigned to the Day of Atonement.

Even these seemingly routine facts begin to reveal the power of *Yom Kippur* and its ultimate fulfillment. Then, with that foundation, we will dig deeply into the atonement ritual, discovering the Cross in the midst of the desert.

Please note that some questions in this study are marked with this symbol: ✳. These are personal questions, and you will not be expected to share your responses in a group study setting, unless you would like to do so.

Day One

Leviticus 16

Vayikra. And He called.

It is the first Hebrew word of Leviticus, and its meaning is a

central theme throughout the book. Over and over, Moses emphasizes

the fact that God Himself is calling and

reaching out to His Chosen. That is why

in Judaism, Leviticus is often called

> Then the Lord called to
> Moses...saying, "Speak
> to the sons of Israel..."
> Leviticus 1:1-2 NAS

Vayikra. The title is a poignant reminder that in the midst of the Law,

the greatest personal treasure is to simply hear the voice of God.

Leviticus is not just the structural center of the Five Books of

Moses (also called the *Pentateuch*, *Torah*, or the Law). It also represents

> "...all things which are
> written about Me in the
> Law of Moses and the
> Prophets and the Psalms
> must be fulfilled."
> Luke 24:44 NAS

the spiritual center of the entire Jewish faith.

For here, at the core of the Law, we witness

a God who dwells among His people, who

continually speaks to them, and who

instructs His children how to live righteously before Him and

harmoniously with one another.

1. **Read Leviticus 1:1. From where did God speak to the Israelites?** _____

2. **Consider the theme of God's continuous call to the Israelites throughout Leviticus. What does this and #1 say to you about God's relationship to His children?** _____

   _____

   _____

3. **Read the first two verses of each chapter in Leviticus. In a word, what was the Lord sharing with the Israelites?** _____

   _____

4. **What benefits do such explicit societal, spiritual and health guidelines provide to a new nation?**

   _____

   _____

   _____

The meticulous rules in Leviticus weren't meant to be a burden to the Israelites. Instead, they provided structure for a group of exiles preparing to become a godly nation in a pagan land. An embryo of a nation from which God's own Son would one day be born.

Tucked inside the meticulously detailed ordinances of Leviticus, the sixteenth chapter reveals God's instructions for the Day of Atonement, or *Yom Kippur*. Here, God calls to His children, inviting them to be reconciled to Himself through the shedding of perfect, atoning blood.

5. **As a foundation for our study, read Leviticus 16 in your Bible. Identify the following aspects of the Day of Atonement ritual:**

    a. The person conducting the ritual _____

    b. The three animals _____

    c. The purpose each animal serves _____
    _____
    _____

6. **Read Leviticus 23:27. What is the holy day called?** _____
    _____

    Our English bibles call *Yom Kippur* the "Day of Atonement."
While this is technically correct, something is lost in the translation. *Yom*
is straightforward; it means "day." So it's the Day of *Kippur*. The noun
not only means atonement, but also expiation and ransom. Put together,
the words provide a much deeper understanding of what happens on this
day: the sins of God's children are paid for and they are erased by the
payment of a ransom.

    In Leviticus 16, the Lord also uses a verb form of *kippur* to
demonstrate *how* we are actually brought into this state of reconciliation
with Him. This verb, *kaphar*, paints the picture in even richer detail.

7. **What are the key verbs used in the second phrase of the following passages? (Use different translations for comparison if you have them available.)**

    a. Leviticus 16:6 _____

b. Genesis 6:14 _____

c. Isaiah 6:7 _____

In Leviticus 16:16, God instructs the High Priest to *make atonement* for the people. In Genesis 6:14, He instructs Noah to *cover* the ark with pitch, making it watertight. And in Isaiah 6:7, the angel *purges* the prophet of his sin with the touch of a burning coal to his lips. These verbs are all the exact same Hebrew word: *kaphar*. Taking these Scriptures together, then, God leads us to understand that His atonement ritual covers and seals our sins completely, forever purging them from who we are in His eyes. And, according to Leviticus 16, this atoning cover must be the blood of a perfect sacrifice brought into His very Presence.

8. **With this brief first reading of our text, how do you see the Cross foreshadowed in this, the Lord's original atonement ritual?** _____
   _____
   _____
   _____
   _____

Day Two

The Nature of Sin

That there is a Day of Atonement at all attests to the fact that people are sinful. But what exactly is sin? Most people don't like to discuss it—the word sounds judgmental and, well, *mean*. Words like *misconduct, mistakes, and mischief* are so much more palatable to us than *sin*. Or *sinful*. Or, even worse, *sinner*. But perhaps this is because we have lost touch with what sin really is. So let's

> "You shall be clean from all your sins before the Lord."
>
> Leviticus 16:30 NAS

check our baggage at the door and examine what sin truly is, specifically in the eyes of God. For when we do, it only magnifies the depth of His love for us.

1. **Review Leviticus 16. Who is exempt from the atonement ritual? What does this say to you?** _____
   _____
   _____
   _____

   In the Old Testament, there are four primary words for sin (plus their derivatives). Not coincidentally, the Lord uses all four of them in His discussion of the Day of Atonement in Leviticus 16.

And [the high priest] shall make atonement for the holy place, because of the impurities (tumah) of the sons of Israel, and because of their transgressions (pesha)...Then Aaron shall lay both of his hands on the head of the live goat, and confess over it all the iniquities (avon) of the sons of Israel...You shall be clean from all your sins (chatta'ah) before the Lord. Leviticus 16:16a, 21a, 30b

2. **Below are other Scriptures containing the Hebrew words for sin used in Leviticus 16. Look up the verses and match them with their appropriate meaning(s) (some have more than one meaning, and some meanings are used more than once).**

Tumah (**and root** *tamei*)	a. Rebellion against God
Psalm 106:39a _____	
Ezekiel 20:7 _____	b. Physical uncleanness
Pesha (**and root** *pasha*)	c. Specific sin/breaking God's law
Job 34:37 _____	
Psalm 5:10 _____	
	d. Breach of relationship
Avon	
Deut 19:15 _____	e. Idolatry
Gen 4:13 _____	
	f. Punishment of sin
Chatta'ah (**and root** *chata*)	
Leviticus 4:2 _____	g. Falling short of God's standard
Leviticus 5:15 _____	
1 Samuel 19:4 _____	h. Sum of past misdeeds

Many consider *tumah's* root, *tamei*, to be the most significant word

in Leviticus. It literally means to be morally or ceremonially foul. And,

while *tamei* often refers to physical impurity, the most serious form is idolatry—putting anything, or anyone, ahead of God. One Jewish scholar describes it as a "moral state akin to radioactivity."[4]

Pasha and *avon* are equally serious. *Pasha* is a "premeditated crossing of the line of God's law, a rebellious act of rejecting God's authority,"[5] and *avon* is wickedness, rebellion or iniquities. *Avon* often refers to the sum of past misdeeds against both God and man, encompassing both the deed and its punishment or consequence.[6]

3. ✳ **Consider whether there is anything taking priority over your focus on the Lord (idolatry), or if any rebellion is currently distancing you from Him.** _____

_____

_____

_____

Finally, *chatta'ah* is derived from *chata*, the most important[7] and common Hebrew word for sin. In almost every case, it refers to a specific sin or to an offering that atones for a sin. It is similar to the Greek word *hamartano*, both of which mean, primarily, to miss, fail, or be off target—falling short of the standard of God's holiness and perfection.

> For all have sinned (hamartano) and fallen short of the glory of God.
>
> Romans 3:23

Does the word "sin" seem more tangible now? Our inevitable human pollution and radioactive idolatry (*tamei*) is unholy enough. But it also leads us to willful disobedience against our Creator (*pesha*), which heaps upon us the full sum of all these misdeeds and their fitting consequences (*avon*). And, lest anyone try to argue that they have never sinned or rebelled against God, *chata* reminds us, simply, that only God is perfectly and eternally sinless; the rest of us, then, are by default tainted or stained or steeped in sin. It is the accumulation of all this internal and external grime that drives the need for the *Yom Kippur* sacrifice.

In some ways, this understanding of sin should bring us some sense of relief. Calling myself a sinner doesn't mean I'm any worse—or better—than the next person. But this understanding of sin must also bring a sense of conviction. For, no matter how "good" a person we may be, our goodness will never get us into God's Presence, because—with our human hearts and human natures—we're still mired in sin. We are all in need of the atoning cover of perfect blood.

> If we claim to be without sin, we deceive ourselves.
>
> I John 1:8

Day Three

The Tenth of Tishri

Tishri 10.

It is the scriptural date for the Day of Atonement—the tenth day of the seventh month.[a] The date is not arbitrary at all. In fact, the date God assigned to *Yom Kippur* points powerfully both to Israel's past and to its messianic future. You see, according to rabbinic scholars, two incredibly significant events occurred on Tishri 10, long before the Lord assigned it to the Day of Atonement.

> "The tenth day of this seventh month is the Day of Atonement."
> Leviticus 23:27

1. **What event does Exodus 32:1-6 record?** _____

2. **Read Exodus 32:7-10. What was God's initial reaction?** ____
    _____

3. **Read Exodus 32:14. How did He ultimately respond?** _____
    _____

4. **Read Exodus 32:14-19. Did God extend His forgiveness before or after the Israelites asked for it?** _____

---

[a] According to Scripture, the Feast of Trumpets and *Yom Kippur* fall on the first and tenth days of the *seventh* month, respectively. During later Biblical history, Tishri became relabeled as the *first* month. As a result, because it was now the first day of the first month, the Feast of Trumpets gained the name *Rosh Hashanah*, or "Head of the Year."

As the Lord's anger burned against His fickle, ungrateful children,

Moses pleaded on their behalf. And God, in His amazing grace, put

aside His anger and forgave them. Even more incredible is the fact that

He extended His forgiveness *before* the people were even confronted with

their sin, while they were still reveling in the midst of their idolatry.

The Talmud [b] teaches that the very day on which Moses brought

the second set of tablets to the Israelites—confirming God's

forgiveness—was none other than Tishri 10.[8]

5. **Do you see a parallel between God's forgiveness of the
    Israelites and His forgiveness of us through Christ? If so, what
    is it?** _____

    _____
    _____
    _____

Jesus died for our pardon without us even asking for it, without

us even knowing we needed it. The truth is, we don't have a clue how

> But God demonstrates
> His own love for us in
> this: while we were still
> sinners, Christ died for us.
> Romans 5:8

much we are in need of God's forgiveness

until after we have received it. And even

then, we still can't comprehend it fully.

---

[b] The Talmud, which means *study*, is a collection of oral commentary and interpretation of the
Law begun under Ezra's Great Assembly. With the destruction of the Temple in 70 A.D., rabbis
began the task of writing down these oral traditions and rulings, which are still relied on today.

But the Lord went one step further. With the date he chose for *Yom Kippur*, He did more than just remind us that He is waiting to forgive us before we even ask. By ordaining the Day of Atonement on the tenth of Tishri, He also gave us a vivid picture of exactly *how* He was going to extend forgiveness. And herein lies a second, breathtaking glimpse at how unarbitrary God's calendar is.

6. **Read Genesis 22:1-19. What event does this passage describe?**
   _____

7. **In what way does this event point to *Yom Kippur*, the Day of Atonement?** _____
   _____
   _____

8. **How does this event point to the Cross?** _____
   _____
   _____

Judaism teaches that Abraham and Isaac experienced their most memorable day of faith and salvation on the *tenth of Tishri*. On the day that would later become the Day of Atonement, aging Abraham obeyed his Lord's command to sacrifice his only son. Until, of course, the angel of the Lord cried out to stay Abraham's obedient raised hand. By establishing *Yom Kippur* on Tishri 10, God forever marked the anniversary of His substitution on Isaac's behalf. For Abraham and

Isaac, and for Moses and the Israelites, this date would forever remind them of the Most High's mercy and His acceptance of a substitute in place of their own blood. *The Creator simply does not want His children to die.*

The Lord's choice of Tishri 10 must do more on the Day of Atonement than turn our eyes back to Moses and to Abraham and Isaac. By turning our attention to what He had already done, the Lord also painted a picture of what He would do in the future. For, thirty-three generations later,

> But God demonstrates His own love for us in this: while we were still sinners, Christ died for us.
> Romans 5:8

in the shadow of Herod's Temple, our Heavenly Father was not only willing, but *did* sacrifice His only Son as the ransom for us all. And through that perfect Sacrifice, all of mankind was extended unconditional forgiveness, even before we knew we needed it.

9. ✳ **Reflect on your own relationship with God. When and how did you realize your need for Him and His grace?** _____

_____

_____

_____

_____

_____

_____

Day Four
The Blood Requirement

Amazingly, despite our unclean nature and sinful actions, God

desires to be united with the children He created. This reunion requires

atonement for sin and purification from the tainted nature that separates

us from Him in the first place. Thus, the

book of Leviticus. It is here that God

demands a price for sin. Sacrifice must be

made, and it must be made with blood.

> "For the life of the flesh is in the blood, and I have given it to you on the altar to make atonement for your souls."
> Leviticus 17:11 NAS

Leviticus begins with a description of five types of offerings to

God. These five types of sacrifices were conducted numerous times

every single day of the year during the daily worship services [c] and

through the personal offerings of the Israelites.

1. **Skim Leviticus 1-5. What were the five types of offerings?** _
   _____
   _____

2. **Which appear to be voluntary and which are demanded by God?** _____
   _____
   _____

---

[c] Numbers 28 sets forth the order and type of sacrifices for the daily worship service.

3.   What set apart the sin and guilt offerings from the others?

_____

_____

4.   What differences do you see between the guilt and sin offerings? _____

_____

_____

_____

The burnt offering was the standard sacrifice, often preceding other sacrifices. This worship offering was to be wholly consumed by fire,[d] symbolizing complete surrender to God by the offeror. The grain offering was brought either by itself or in combination with burnt and peace offerings, but never with guilt or sin offerings. The peace/fellowship offering was a sacrifice of completion, always following another sacrifice. This most joyous of all sacrifices indicated a state of peace with God.

As worshipful as the burnt, grain and peace offerings were, they did not deal with sin, nor were they specifically required outside of the

> Without the shedding of blood there is no forgiveness.
> Hebrews 9:22b

daily worship routine. In contrast, the guilt and sin offerings were obligatory, required by God in order to be reconciled to Him and others.

---

[d] It is powerful to note that the Greek rendering of _olah_ (the burnt offering, literally "that which goes up") is _holokauston_, translated in English as holocaust.

Such reconciliation required bloodshed.

The guilt offering was one of reparation, often made in conjunction with financial or material restitution to the offended party. But the sin offering was considered the most important of all sacrifices. It is often referred to as a purification or "de-sin" offering, because its purpose was to cleanse the sinner. One scholar describes the blood of the sin sacrifice "as a detergent to absorb and purify the pollution...[of] humanness."[9] As we will see later on, a very special sin offering is the focal point of the Day of Atonement ritual.

> "This annual atonement must be made with the blood of the atoning sin offering for the generations to come. It is most holy to the Lord."
>
> Exodus 30:10

A key difference between the guilt and sin offerings is perhaps best explained by Edersheim: "the trespass (guilt) offering may be regarded as representing ransom for a specific wrong, while the sin offering symbolized general redemption [of the person]."[10]

But why was an annual sin offering required on *Yom Kippur*, if the Israelites had been bringing personal ones throughout the year? Good question. For some perspective, let us consider the well-known gospel account of Jesus washing the disciples' feet on the eve of His crucifixion.

5. **Read John 13:6-10. How could Jesus' explanation to Peter relate to the Old Testament sin offerings versus the annual** *Yom Kippur* **offering made in God's Presence?** _____

_____

_____

_____

6. **How could it relate to what Jesus accomplished on the Cross for us?** _____

_____

_____

_____

Each year, the Israelites were bathed in God's forgiveness through the blood of the perfect *Yom Kippur* lamb. Then, throughout the year, their personal sin offerings washed away the sins of daily life. Today, if you are in Christ, your very soul was cleansed by the blood of

> Wash away all my iniquity and cleanse me from my sin…Cleanse me with hyssop, and I will be clean; wash me, and I will be whiter than snow.
>
> Psalm 51:2,7

the perfect Lamb when you first received Him. Then, through your continual confessions, He continues to wash away the spiritual and emotional grime you accumulate walking through this world each day.

7. ✻ **What "grime"—sins—are you in need of having cleansed by Christ today? Own them and confess them to Him now, that you might walk more closely with Him.** _____

_____

_____

_____

Day Five

A Sabbath of Sabbaths

The Day of *Atonement*. The one day each year on which the Most

Holy God erased every single charge against His devoted children. A day

on which perfect blood paid the ransom for

those sins. A day that, through the key events

God memorialized with *Yom Kippur*'s date,

> "It is to be a
> Sabbath of solemn
> rest for you."
> Leviticus 16:31
> NAS

pointed to the Substitute who would erase mankind's sin once and for all.

Quite a day. It's no wonder that the Lord commanded the

Israelites to observe it as a *Shabbat Shabbaton*. The words sound pretty

important, and they are. Literally, they mean a Sabbath of sacred

Sabbath, a Sabbath of great Sabbath, a Sabbath of solemn Sabbath, or a

Sabbath of complete Sabbath.[11]

1. **Read Leviticus 16:31, Leviticus 23:3, Leviticus 23:24-25,
   Leviticus 23:27-32, and Leviticus 23:34-35,39. Which two
   festivals are identified as *Shabbaton*, or a "rest?"** _____
   _____

2. **Which two are identified as *Shabbat Shabbaton*, or a sabbath of
   rest/complete rest/solemn rest?** _____
   _____

3. **What differences do you note in the observation of a** *Shabbaton* **and a** *Shabbat Shabbaton*? _____

_____

_____

Clearly, the Feast of Trumpets (*Rosh Hashanah*) and the Feast of

Tabernacles (*Sukkot*) are of great importance to the Lord. On these days,

His people ceased from their professional labor. But the weekly Sabbath

and *Yom Kippur* are so sacred to the Lord that He prohibited any type of

work at all, under penalty of banishment and death. A mandatory break

from work and household chores sounds great, doesn't it? But does this

mean we should fill the day with other busy activities in their place?

4. **Read Genesis 8:22, Joshua 5:12a, Psalm 46:9a. What is the key verb in these verses?** _____

5. **Does it indicate (a) a scaling back or (b) a complete cessation?**

The key Hebrew verb in these verses is *shabath*, meaning "to

cease, desist or rest," and it is the root of *shabbath* (Sabbath)—literally

"intermission."[12] To observe the Sabbath we aren't simply to change

our routine, but to cease and desist. *Stop.* Stop *everything* except

worshipping the One who created you and celebrating the blessings He

has given.

Now, I am not advocating legalism. Even Paul, the former

Pharisee, warned against turning the Sabbath into a ritualistic stumbling

block. But when we choose to honor God on His Day, we demonstrate

our trust in Him. Trust that the Hand that set the Earth in orbit can

maximize our job productivity,
help get our shopping done, and
bless our studies when we halt to
honor Him. God will surely bless
the tithe of your time, and you

> "Bring the whole tithe into the storehouse...Test me in this," says the Lord Almighty, "and see if I will not throw open the floodgates of heaven and pour out so much blessing that you will not have room enough for it."
>
> Malachi 3:10

will experience rest like never before.

6. ✳ **Read Isaiah 58:13-14. Consider how you observe the Sabbath. How might you honor God even more on His holy day?** _____

_____

_____

A *Shabbat Shabbaton* is serious business. Yet God elevated *Yom*

Kippur even further. On that day, He required the Israelites to deny

themselves.[13] The Hebrew word, *anah*, literally means to abase, afflict or

chasten oneself.[14] Does this mean that God wants us to beat ourselves

up to the point of hopelessness? Of course not! But nothing produces

greater desperation than looking at ourselves in the bright light of God's

holiness. And this sense of unworthiness is exactly where the Israelites needed to be on the Day of Atonement—and where we all need to be when we consider the Cross. For it is in that place of honest personal accounting that we truly comprehend that God's love is nothing short of a lavish, divine gift.

This afflicting of souls on *Yom Kippur* involves a twenty-four-hour fast. It is the only full day of fasting specifically commanded by God in all of Scripture.[15] In fact, in Acts 27:9, Luke calls it simply "the Fast."

7. **Read 2 Chronicles 20:3 and Ezra 10:6. In the right spirit, what can fasting accomplish?** _____
   _____

8. **How might fasting impact a person's observation of the Day of Atonement?** _____
   _____
   _____

9. ✳ **Have you ever fasted to hear a special word from God? Are you dealing with something right now for which fasting may help you draw nearer to Him?** _____
   _____
   _____
   _____

The Day of Atonement. A *Shabbat Shabbaton*. A cessation of cessations. The Fast of all fasts. From these biblical descriptions alone, we can see that the Day of Atonement is of overwhelming significance to God. As such, it should be of overwhelming significance to us as well.

Week Two

The Architecture of Sin
The Holiest Places

> The Lord spoke to Moses after the death of the two
> sons of Aaron who died when they approached the
> Lord. The Lord said to Moses; "Tell your brother Aaron
> not to come whenever he chooses into the Most Holy
> Place behind the curtain in front of the atonement cover
> on the ark, or else he will die, because I appear in the
> cloud over the atonement cover.
>
> Leviticus 16:1-2

With the opening verses of Leviticus 16 (above), we are reminded

of a dire fact: coming into the presence of God can be deadly. Man's

first sin forced the Creator to withdraw His physical Presence, not out of

anger but out of necessity. His Purity couldn't be tainted by the presence

of impurity. So the first Father could no longer allow Himself to walk

alongside the children He lovingly created. It grieved Him beyond what

we can fathom, but He had no choice.

The Most Holy Lord drove the point home for the rest of His children by establishing an "architecture" of sin: grand, physical barriers in the form of the Tabernacle. Residing within the innermost chamber, the Holy of Holies, the Lord remained inaccessibly separate. Living their lives in daily view of the Tabernacle reminded the Israelites of their sinful estrangement from God. At the same time, however, the sight was also a powerful reminder of the unquenchable love of a Father determined to live among His children—simply because they are His.

There are three key reasons why this architecture is so integral to *Yom Kippur*, the Old Testament Day of Atonement. The first is to remind all of us that we will *never* be pure enough to enter God's Presence on our own. Secondly, the architecture itself played an important role in the atonement ritual, from the outermost entrance straight through every barrier into the very Holy of Holies. Finally, and perhaps most astoundingly, every aspect of the Tabernacle's construction and contents pointed directly to Jesus, the future Messiah who would ultimately abolish every single barrier, guiding each of us by the hand directly into the Presence of our Holy God.

Day One

The Dwelling Place

Let us begin by peering into the very core, the space that the Almighty "occupied:" the Holy of Holies. The Holy of Holies made up the westernmost 15 feet of the Tabernacle—a perfect square.[e] Its only material content was the Ark of the Covenant,[f] but it also "housed" the Living God.

> "Then have them make a sanctuary for me and I will dwell among them."
>
> Exodus 25:8

1. **Read Exodus 25:10-22. Of what two materials was the Ark constructed?** _____

2. **What does your Bible call the lid of the Ark?** _____
    _____

When the Lord gave instructions for the Ark's golden cover, He used a unique Hebrew word, one that refers to this specific article and nothing else in all of Scripture. He called it the *kapporeth*. One would expect that this special name God assigned to the lid would mean the "Throne of Glory," or perhaps the "Holy Seat." After all, His very

---

[e] See page. 160 for a diagram of the desert Tabernacle.

[f] The stone tablets inside the Ark were also called the "Testimony," since they testified to the covenant between the Lord and the Israelites. The Ark later contained some manna and Aaron's budded rod (Numbers 17) as well. Upon the Ark's arrival at Solomon's Temple, however, only the stone tablets remained inside (Hebrews 9:4; Halley, 1965).

Presence would rest there. Maybe in man's economy, but not in God's.

You see, *kapporeth* is derived not from *kadosh*, meaning holy, but from

Kippur, meaning atonement or expiation. The common translation of

> "And there I will
> meet with you; and
> from above the
> mercy seat...I will
> speak to you."
>
> Exodus 25:22

"mercy seat" therefore joins the physical function of the lid (seat) with God's purpose for being there—to grant us mercy. With this word, *kapporeth*, the Lord declared His desire to sit upon

a throne from which to bestow grace upon those who would approach it

in faith.

But there was a catch. A big catch. This Throne of Mercy was

absolutely off-limits because it stood within the Holy of Holies. Just one

step inside would result in death. What, then, was the point of a mercy

seat if no one could plead their case before its Holy Occupant? Well,

there was—of course—one exception: *Yom Kippur*. On this day, the

High Priest was to offer atonement for the nation at God's seat of mercy.

And on this day, God would grant forgiveness not from a distance, but

from His earthly Throne.

3.   **Read 1 Samuel 6:19. What happened when the people of Beth-Shemeth removed the mercy seat from the Ark and looked inside?** _____

_____

4.   How might this relate to salvation in Jesus Christ? _____

_____

_____

_____

If we remove the mercy from God's Throne, we are left looking

only at the stone tablets—the Law. And the Law, without God's mercy,

can only convict us of our sinfulness without providing a remedy.

Graciously, the Lord *did* provide a remedy. In the Tabernacle, God's

Law was literally covered with His seat of mercy. And, centuries later,

the perfect embodiment of the Law walked the earth wrapped in the

flesh of grace. With His death on the Cross, Jesus assured us that,

despite our inability to fulfill the Law, His grace was sufficient, and He

offered it freely.

**5.   ✳ Are you daily relying on God's mercy, or are you seeking the
Law—religious acts—in order to earn His favor on your own?**

_____

_____

_____

_____

**6.   Refer back to today's first question. Of what type of wood was
the Ark constructed?** _____

Acacia, or shittim, grew in the deserts of Sinai and around the

Dead Sea—places where nothing else could grow.[16]   In other words, it was a root out of dry ground. The tree is covered with thorns, and its wood withstands decay.[17] Some acacia pods even yield a substance used for washing delicate silk.[18] And when pierced, the tree's sap is used for medicinal purposes.[19]

He grew up...like a root out of dry ground.
Isaiah 53:2

The soldiers wove a crown of thorns and put it on his head.
John 19:2 NAS

You will not...let your Holy One see decay.
Psalm 16:10

The blood of Jesus His Son cleanses us from all sin.
1 John 1:7 NAS

He was pierced for our transgressions.
Isaiah 53:5

Power was coming from Him and healing them all.
Luke 6:19b

Can't you see it? God's earthy throne of gold rested upon none other than the image of His incarnate Son. Some 1,500 years later, like the acacia, Jesus would wear a crown of thorns at His crucifixion. He would rise from the grave, defeating the decay of death for all eternity. And His blood would flow forth to gently wash with divine healing all who would apply it to themselves.

Oh, approach the throne of glory today!

Day Two

The Veil

Someday, the Divine source of mercy and healing would not be off-limits. But for the Israelites in the desert, it was. And so began the layers of physical separation between God and man. Separating the Holy of Holies from the rest of the Tabernacle, or the Holy Place, hung a veil. This was no ordinary curtain. No, God instructed these desert nomads to weave a brilliant tapestry of blue, purple and scarlet yarn and of finely twisted linen, with images of

> "And you shall make a veil of blue and purple and scarlet material and twisted linen ..."
>
> Exodus 26:31 NAS

cherubim worked into the fabric. Just imagine the process as they painstakingly wove the holy fabric together in the middle of the dusty Sinai.

At 15 feet by 15 feet and three feet thick,[20] the veil certainly served its function of secluding the Holy of Holies. But God is always about more than mere function. While the veil served its purpose to shroud His Presence from the eyes of mortal man, this divider was a breathtaking picture of Who was inside, and Who was yet to come. The Creator was still creating. For, woven together in this tapestry (as well as the tapestries that would make up the walls of the Tabernacle) were rich colors that spoke so much without saying a word.

1. **Look up the verses next to each color/material. What do you think the biblical symbolism of each is?**

    a. *blue*: **Exodus 24:10, Ezekiel 10:1** _____

    b. *red*: **Isaiah 1:18, 2 Kings 3:22** _____

    c. *purple*: **Judges 8:26, Daniel 5:7, Luke 16:19** _____

    d. *linen*: **Revelation 15:6 and 19:8** _____

Every moment that the priests and Levites ministered in the Tabernacle, they were reminded of God's heavenly kingdom and His Spirit by the blue yarn in the veil. They could never forget that the One they served was no ordinary monarch, but the King of Heaven dwelling among men.

Woven in contrast to the blue was the scarlet yarn, reminding the religious leaders of their own sin and the nation's sin, as well as the blood required to atone for them. Surely it cannot be

> "Though your sins are... red (adam) as crimson, they shall be like wool."
>
> Isaiah 1:18

mere coincidence that the Hebrew word for red, derived from the word for blood (*dam*, pronounced dahm), is also the name of the very first man: *adam*.

Running through the blue and scarlet was the purple thread, proclaiming God's royalty and His wealth. Yet this color of majesty was itself symbolic of something even deeper.

2. **How is purple created?** _____

3. **Given the symbolism of blue and of red, what could their combination be communicating to the Israelites then and to us today?** _____
_____
_____

The King of Kings allowed the color of heaven (blue) to mingle with the color of man and sacrifice (red), a picture of His determination to live alongside His children. But the colors also painted a picture of the lengths this Creator would go to in order to do so. This blending of blue and red provided an early glimpse of Jesus, the perfect union of heaven and man. The One who came from Heaven to shed earthly blood in order to put aside the veil's division forever.

Finally, delicately woven into these rich, heavy colors was linen, a symbol of righteousness and purity. It reminded the Israelites that, although this heavenly Monarch dwells in the midst of sinful men, He— and His coming Anointed—is altogether pure and righteous, and must therefore remain separated from them.

The linen surrounding God's Presence in that Holy of Holies also provided a prophetic glimpse of the cloth that, 1,500 years later, would briefly shroud the lifeless body of Jesus, the final Atonement. The perfect Sacrifice of heaven and earth that would literally render the veil useless.

4. **The writer of Hebrews teaches that Jesus' body, His very flesh, became the veil between God and man, ultimately giving us access to the Almighty.**

    Offer praise to the Lord by writing various aspects of Christ's nature and sacrifice on the "veil" below.

Blue	Red	Purple	Linen

> ...by a new and living way opened for us through the curtain, that is, his body.
>
> Hebrews 10:20

Day Three

The Altar of Incense

On the other side of the majestic veil, completing the Tabernacle,

was the Holy Place, an area seemingly too large—30feet by 15 feet—for

just three small objects: the Altar of Incense, the table for the Bread of

the Presence, and the golden Lampstand, or *menorah*. The Altar of

Incense stood just outside the veil, and played a

key role in the *Yom Kippur* ritual.

"Make an altar of acacia wood for burning incense."

Exodus 30:1

The altar measured just 18 inches square

and three feet high. Yet, constructed of acacia wood covered with gold,

the small altar provided yet another vivid image of the earthly Christ

overlaid with the richness of His Heavenly kingship.

1. **Read Exodus 30:7-8 in your Bible. How often was the High Priest to burn incense on the altar?** _____

2. **Read Exodus 30:9-10. Other than the holy incense, what was the only thing to be offered on the Altar of Incense? On what occasion?** _____

3. **Read Exodus 30:34. What are the four ingredients in the holy incense?** _____

4. **Based on your existing knowledge, how did any of these ingredients point to Christ?** _____

_____

The Magi's gifts to the newborn Savior of frankincense and myrrh (or "stacte") were a kind of benediction—"May your life rise in a pleasing aroma to Your Father the King." They also consecrated the Prince of Peace to His ultimate mission: the myrrh bestowed upon Jesus at His mortal birth would later anoint Him in His mortal death (see John 19:39). But these substances didn't just play a role in Jesus' life, they also painted a vivid picture of what that life would be like, long before it ever came to pass.

5. **Consider these facts about the incense ingredients.**

Onycha was derived from a shellfish living in the Red Sea.[21] The shell "need[ed] to be beaten into a very fine powder."[22]

Galbanum is a pungent resin from the Ferula shrub, which grows in the Syrian mountains and along the Mediterranean.[23] It is used primarily as a preservative for the aroma of other ingredients.[24]

Frankincense is not only used for fragrance, but also for medicinal purposes. Frankincense is actually a stimulant, used throughout history to treat everything from tumors to laryngitis to leprosy.[25] It is still used even today for its antiseptic, antifungal, and anti-inflammatory properties.[26]

Myrrh (stacte), galbanum and frankincense were all resins obtained by piercing the stem of their respective plants.[27]

Now read Psalm 16:10, Isaiah 53:5, Matthew 9:35 and Matthew 27:26, 30. Share what you see in the fragrant mixture.

_____

_____

_____

The images of Jesus' life, death and resurrection in the holy incense ingredients is almost too much to take in. But the vision of Christ does not end there. You see, there is much more to collecting frankincense than a simple piercing. After first piercing the *Bosweillia Thurifera* tree, gatherers let the initial drip harden from exposure to the air.[28] Then they make a second, deeper incision. From this second incision, clear, yellowish "tears" form (yes, they are called tears, as in weeping). After three months, the tears are collected and ground into pure frankincense.

Jesus was literally the living Holy Incense. His life continually rose up in a

> Christ... gave himself up for us, an offering and a sacrifice to God as a fragrant aroma.
>
> Ephesians 5:2 NAS

pleasing aroma to His Father as He worked spiritual and physical healing on earth. His touch and His words restored the leper, gave voice to the mute, and even brought the dead to life.

Even so, the Messiah was beaten and crushed, just like the sweet

onchya. And then, upon a tree, the Anointed was pierced first in His hands and feet, and later a second time, deep into His side, bringing forth a flow of blood and water. Tears of mourning flowed from the hearts of His disciples. Yet after three days these tears were collected and transformed into pure joy as Jesus defeated the decay of death. The perfectly preserved, incorruptible One rose and ascended to His rightful place in the Heavens.

It is overwhelming to think that even as the Israelites wandered in the desert—and later worshipped in Solomon's Temple—Heaven was filled with the aroma of Christ and His future sacrifice as the son of the Most High.

6. ✳ **Read Revelation 5:8. Let your praise and wonder for God's perfect ways be swept up to the Throne of Heaven.** _____

_____
_____
_____
_____

May my prayer be set before You like incense. Psalm 141:2

Day Four

The Bread of the Presence

One would think that the symbolism of the incense would be enough, but the Lord had even more to say in His design of the Holy Place. There was to be absolutely no mistaking the Man who would one day come to replace God's earthly dwelling with His own Flesh. And so, on the north side of the Holy Place sat another small square table (also 18 inches square). This table displayed the Bread of the Presence or the Shewbread. The bread served as a reminder to the Israelites of both the Lord's physical and spiritual sustenance to them.

> "Put the Bread of the Presence on this table to be before me at all times."
>
> Exodus 25:30

1. **Read Exodus 25:23-30. Visualize the setting, and share how the table was prepared.** _____
    _____
    _____

2. **Read Leviticus 24:5-8. How was the bread presented? What do you think the number of loaves signified?** _____
    _____
    _____
    _____

These verses give us a great visual image of what the bread and its

table look like. But the *name* God chose for the twelve loaves actually

gave the Israelites—and us—a picture of what *He Himself* looks like.

Your Bible probably calls it the Shewbread or Bread of the

Presence. The Hebrew words are "*lechem*" (bread) *paniym*." *Paniym*

literally means "face," "presence," or "person." The fascinating thing is

that, while *paniym* is a plural noun, it is always used in the singular. In

other words, Shewbread could be accurately translated as "bread of the

faces that make up one face" or, even further, "bread of the persons that

May the grace of the Lord **Jesus** Christ, and the love of **God**, and the fellowship of the **Holy Spirit** be with you all. 2 Corinthians 13:14 *(emphasis added)*	make up the one person." In the very name for this holy bread, the Lord shed glorious light on His compound nature—the Three that make up the One whole.

Interestingly, even Jewish history teaches that the Shewbread was

symbolic of the Messiah to come.[29] What, then, did the bread tell the

Israelites about their future Savior?

3. **Read Exodus 25:23-24. Of what materials was the Shewbread table constructed?** _____

4. **Read Leviticus 24:5-7. What was sprinkled on the loaves?**

_____

5. **Read Leviticus 8:26a and 1 Corinthians 5:6-8. What ingredient was to be omitted from the holy bread? How did this point to the coming Christ?** _____

_____

6. **Together with the other lessons of this week, what did these details about the Shewbread and its table reveal abut the life and death of Jesus, the Messiah yet to come?** _____

_____

_____

   Each of the twelve loaves was sprinkled with the image of the suffering Christ, and they sat upon a table whose materials symbolized this same indestructible Servant King of Heaven. Jewish writings even tell us that the loaves were anointed with oil—in the form of a cross![30] And, while these materials provided a glimpse of how the Messiah would die, the omission of yeast also foretold how Jesus would live—completely without sin.

> Let us keep the Festival, not with the old yeast, the yeast of malice and wickedness, but with bread without yeast, the bread of sincerity and truth.
>
> I Corinthians 5:8

7. **Read Leviticus 24:8-9. How often and when were the loaves replaced?** _____

_____

8. **What was done with the "outgoing" bread?** _____

_____

Just as the Shewbread fed the priests—God's servants, Jesus came to earth as the Bread of Life for all who would partake of Him—His priesthood of believers.

What amazing prophecies were revealed through the Shewbread's name, ingredients, and presentation! On a daily basis, the holy bread reminded God's twelve tribes of His continual sustenance. And, at the same time, the Lord pointed centuries ahead, to when His children would literally come face-to-Face with the Person

> "I am the living bread that came down from heaven. If anyone eats of this bread, he will live forever. This bread is my flesh, which I will give for the life of the world."
>
> John 6:51

who would nourish, fulfill and sustain their very souls for all eternity.

9. ✳ **Are you feeling weak and malnourished in your spirit today? Feast on the Living Bread and regain your strength—His strength. What nourishment will you seek from Him this day?**

_____

_____

_____

_____

Day Five

The Golden Lampstand

The third and final item in the Holy Place was the golden

lampstand, or *menorah*, which stood on the south side, opposite the Bread

of the Presence. This candelabra provided

the only source of light within the darkened

Tabernacle, which was covered entirely by the

woven tapestries and animal skins that made

up its walls and ceiling.[g]

> The lampstand was made exactly like the pattern the Lord had shown Moses.
>
> Numbers 8:4b

1. **Read Exodus 25:31-40. Of what solid material was the lampstand made?** _____

2. **What food were the branches shaped like?** _____

Often called the "wakeful tree,"[31] the almond tree is the first to

show signs of life in the Near East,[32] blooming in January and bearing

fruit in March[33] while other trees still stand bare in the midst of winter's

sleep. In other words, almonds could literally be considered the

firstfruits of the dead!

---

g We will study these outer coverings during next week's lesson.

3. **Read Exodus 27:20. What was the fuel for the lamps, and how was it made?** _____

    _____

    _____

4. **Look up Matthew 26:36 and Mark 14:32. Does your Bible define the word "Gethsemane?" If so, what is its meaning?**

    _____

5. **Read the following verses and reflect on how the method of shaping the golden lampstand pointed to Christ, the light of the world. Exodus 25:31; Numbers 8:4; Matthew 26:67; and Mark 14:65.** _____

    _____

    _____

    _____

The lamps were to remain lit at all times, fueled by the oil of

crushed olives. Did you know that *Gethsemane* means oil press? It makes

perfect logical sense. After all, the garden sits at the bottom of the

Mount of Olives. For centuries, countless gallons of olive oil were likely

pressed out there for the Lord's service. But the name also made perfect

prophetic sense, because it was here that

our Jesus knelt at the oil press, Himself

crushed in spirit to the point of sweating

> But the Lord was
> pleased to crush Him.
> Isaiah 53:10 NAS

blood.[34] And in Gethsemane, Jesus overlooked the city that, the next

day, would see Him beaten. Indeed, just as the golden lampstand was to

be beaten from its base to its blossoms (Numbers 8:4), the Light of the

World was crushed and beaten from the nail hammered through His feet to the thorny crown pressed into the flesh of His brow. And why? That He might become the true Source of eternal light for all mankind.

6. **Re-read Exodus 25:31-40. What were the measurements of the lampstand?** _____

7. **What does this reveal about the world's Source of Light?** __
   _____

8. **Read Exodus 25:34. What might these four cups signify?** __
   _____

9. **✳ Read Revelation 21:23. Record your thoughts.** _____
   _____
   _____
   _____

In the midst of God's detailed instructions—down to the last carved almond—no measurements were given for the lampstand. How odd, considering how meticulously the Lord marked out every other

> The light shines in the darkness, and the darkness has not overcome it.
>
> John 1:5 KJV

aspect of the Tabernacle. Yet it also makes perfect sense. For, you see, the light of God's Son is immeasurable and infinite, just as John attests in the prologue to his gospel. Christ's light is boundless, extending to the four corners of the earth. Close your eyes and just imagine it: in Heaven, the Glory emanating from God and His Son will be so radiant that it will literally illuminate the entire Kingdom—no sun, no moon, just pure, Divine Light.

Let's close this week by pointing this Light at ourselves.

10. **Read Exodus 30:7. How often were the wicks of the lamps trimmed?** _____

11. **How does the trimming of the wicks relate to the life of a Christian? (See John 15:2 and 1 Thessalonians 5:5)** _____
_____
_____
_____

The priests trimmed the wicks of the golden lampstand daily to prevent waste material from hindering bright, even light.[35] In the same way, God prunes those of us who Jesus now calls the children of light.[36] As the branches of the True Vine, then, we should pray to be trimmed, so that we may grow upward without hindrance and without impurity, glorifying our Source and bringing His Light to all mankind.

> "Every branch that does bear fruit he prunes so that it will be even more fruitful."
> John 15:2

12. ✳ **What is hindering you from shining today? Will you allow the Holy Spirit to cut it away, that you may grow stronger and brighter than ever before?** _____
_____
_____

Week Three

The Architecture of Sin: Surrounded

> Better is one day in your courts than a thousand elsewhere;
> I would rather be a doorkeeper in the house of my God
> than dwell in the tents of the wicked.
>
> Psalm 84:10

Last week, we explored the rich materials and objects that

surrounded the very Presence of the Almighty in the midst of the desert

Tabernacle. Everything—the Ark of the Testimony, the veil, the Altar of

Incense, the Bread of the Presence, and the golden Lampstand—

demonstrated in rich symbolism the suffering, the sustenance, and the

eternal Glory of God's Son, His Anointed, His Jesus.

Do you remember the veil—that tapestry of blue, scarlet, purple

and linen? Well, enveloping the entire Tabernacle, from roof to ground,

were ten just like it, joined together with clasps of gold, draping over the

entire structure. Could you imagine ministering in such a place? As a

priest entered the Tabernacle, he left behind the sandy desert with its unrelenting sun, and entered God's house, surrounded above and around by the magnificent tapestry, lit simply by the flickering of pure oil burning in the seven golden lamps. I can't begin to imagine a more incredible oasis.

The Tabernacle refreshed and inspired body and soul. And its contents proclaimed the holiness of the Heavenly Father, all the while whispering of the Holy One who would one day step out of Heaven and walk among us.

But the messianic foreshadowing wasn't limited to the *inside* of the Tabernacle. Its exterior components and underlying structure pointed vividly to the coming Christ as well. This week, then, we will study four aspects of the Tabernacle's structure: (1) its foundation; (2) its coverings; (3) the two lone objects in the expansive courtyard; and (4) the gate that separated God's desert "home" from His people.

Day One

A Firm Foundation

Very often, what you don't see is more vital than what you do see.

The unseen is what allows the visible to maintain its strength and focus,

whether it is a person's character or a building's

foundation. The Tabernacle is no exception.

The foundation and building materials of the

structure held it together, and their messianic

symbolism pointed to the strong foundation of

our faith—the coming Christ.

> "See, I lay a stone in Zion, a tested stone, a precious cornerstone for a sure foundation: the one who trusts will never be dismayed."
>
> Isaiah 28:16

1. **Read Exodus 36:20-36. What material served as the framework of the Tabernacle?** _____

2. **What material made up the bases for the beams?** _____

3. **Read Psalm 12:6. What could this tell us about the foundation of the Tabernacle?** _____
_____

The Psalmist equates God's Word with refined silver. And he

was right. Tested by the trials of life, God's Word is proven as the

flawless Truth. And the material of this flawless Truth formed the

foundation of His desert dwelling, just as they are the foundation of the entire world, and of our individual lives. This metal of truth supported

beams of acacia, wood which pointed to the One who would later be

revealed as the framework of God's plan and of His body of believers.

Yet there is further meaning in the use of silver here.

4. **Read Exodus 30:11-13 and 38:25-28. How was most of the silver for the Tabernacle obtained?** _____

5. **What do you suppose most biblical scholars therefore identify as silver's symbolic meaning?** _____

The builders obtained the silver from the redemption money

God demanded of every Israelite. So the very currency of atonement

served as the foundation for the Tabernacle.

Just as Christ, our atonement, was slain from

the foundation of the world. Just as Christ,

> ...the Lamb slain from the foundation of the world.
>
> Revelation 13:8 KJV

our atonement, is the foundation of the church of believers. And just as

Christ, our atonement, is the foundation of all our hopes.

6. **Read Revelation 21:9-21. What is made of silver in the New Jerusalem?** _____

7. **What could be the significance of this, given #7 above?** _____

_____
_____
_____

As the currency of redemption, there is absolutely no need for silver in the future New Jerusalem. Why not? Because the transaction will have already taken place. Everyone there has already been atoned for, redeemed with the blood of the Messiah!

In the Gospels we see that silver played another, more sinister, role. The same silver that formed the foundation of the Lord's Tabernacle set the crucifixion event in motion—the foundation, if you will, of the Cross.

8. **Read Matthew 26:14-16. Reflect on the chief priests' use of the sanctuary shekel—the Israelites' atonement or redemption money—as payment for Judas' betrayal of Jesus.** _____
   _____
   _____

9. **Read Matthew 27:3-6. Reflect on the chief priests' refusal to put the silver back into the Temple treasury.** _____
   _____
   _____
   _____

Isn't it ironic that the chief priests found it acceptable to offer the sanctuary shekel to Judas in order to have Jesus killed, yet it was not "lawful" to return it to the Temple coffers. Even so, it is quite fitting that the Jews' redemption money—their silver—was used to set in motion the events that would bring redemption to them and to all of

mankind.

10. Read Exodus 38:9-20. What metal served as the base, or foundation, of the courtyard, outside of God's dwelling? ____

_____

11. Bible scholars teach that bronze symbolizes judgment. What meaning could this lend to #12? _____

_____

Bronze withstands temperatures up to 1675° Fahrenheit without

melting, which makes it the perfect substance to support the courtyard

where burnt offerings were made day in and day out. And bronze's

symbolism of judgment is fitting for an area of sacrifice. Yet the fact that

it served as the foundation *outside* of God's dwelling should not be lost on

us: Living outside of God's Presence, outside of the Truth and

atonement of His Son, will only bring us into judgment. And judgment,

without the solid ground of Christ's redemption on which to stand, is a

fiery place indeed.

12. ✳ Where are you choosing to stand today? _____

_____
_____
_____
_____

Day Two

Covered with the Incorruptible

It's a pity that, after dedicating their possessions and their labor to creating God's majestic Tabernacle, the Israelites could no longer view it. For, draped over the entire structure, protecting the magnificent woven tapestries that made up the Tabernacle's walls and ceiling, were three outer coverings, completely enshrouding the sanctuary.

> He reveals deep and hidden things; He knows what lies in darkness, and light dwells with Him.
>
> Daniel 2:22

The outer coverings obviously served to protect the majestic—and costly—House of God. But they also reflect on the *Yom Kippur* sacrifice and hold some intriguing messianic symbolism in themselves.

1. **Read Exodus 26:7,14. Of what animal skins were the three outer coverings made?** _____

2. **Read Hebrews 11:37. What do we learn about goat skins, the layer closest to the divine dwelling?** _____
   _____

3. **Recall our brief introduction to *Yom Kippur*. What is the goat's key role in the atonement ritual?** _____
   _____

4. **Reflect on how these goat skins may speak to the Day of Atonement ritual and to the coming Cross.** _____

_____

_____

_____

Goat skins were worn by the poor, and represented extreme poverty throughout Scripture.[37] Yet goats were also among the chief possessions of the wealthy during the early ages.[38] So in these skins, we see a union of humility and wealth. In the same way, our Christ was Himself the King of Glory who cloaked Himself in humility to walk among us.

> "Then [Aaron] shall slaughter the goat of the sin offering which is for the people, and bring its blood inside the veil."
>
> Leviticus 16:15 NAS

And, just as the skin of goats was given to cover the sanctuary, Christ Jesus ultimately offered up His own flesh to cover us all.

5. **Read Genesis 22:13 and Leviticus 5:15. What symbolism do you think rams have in Judaism and the Old Testament?** ___

_____

6. **Why do you suppose God commanded that the ram skins for the Tabernacle covering be dyed red?** _____

_____

7. **Read Leviticus 23:23-24 and Leviticus 16:3,22. How do rams hail the beginning and end of the annual atonement process?**

_____

_____

_____

Since the near-sacrifice of Isaac, rams have been considered by

Jews to be symbolic of God's willingness to accept a substitute in our

With trumpets and
the blast of the
ram's horn shout
triumphantly in the
presence of the
Lord, our King…for
He is coming to
judge the earth…

Psalm 98:6,9 HCSB

stead. Ten days before *Yom Kippur*, on *Rosh*

Hashanah, the story of Abraham and Isaac is retold,

and the horn of Isaac's substitute is blown to lead

hearts to repentance (Leviticus 23:23-24). Then

finally, when the atonement ritual was finished, the

burnt offering of a ram demonstrated its completion.

In the desert, then, each time the Israelites packed up and

reassembled the Tabernacle during their wandering, the red ram skins

reminded them that their scarlet sin blocked their access to God. It

reminded them that their sin demanded blood payment. And it

reminded them that, mercifully, the Lord would accept a substitute in

their stead.

8. **Refer back to #1. What animal's skin served as the outermost
    layer of the Tabernacle's protection, according to your Bible
    translation?** _____

9. **Based on the type of animal it is, what might be its purpose as
    the outermost layer?** _____

Depending on your translation, Exodus 26:14 tells of an outer

covering made from the skins of the East African sea cow, dugongs from the Red Sea, dolphins, porpoises, manatees or badgers. The Hebrew word for this animal is *tehashim*, and the truth is that scholars really don't know what it was. We can deduce, though, that since these are all animals living in, or spending considerable time in, the water, their skins provided a watertight covering for the sanctuary. This outermost covering protected God's pure Presence from the elements of the world.

So when God's people looked to the Tabernacle on the Day of Atonement, they could only see a drab waterproof cover, not the Glory that resided within. Yet, you will recall that *kaphar*, the word describing Noah's perfect sealing of the ark, is the same word for "make atonement" in Leviticus 16. And so, on the Day of Atonement, the waterproof skin reminded the people that the blood being sprinkled at that very moment covered their sin perfectly—at least for another year.

Ultimately on the Cross, the perfect Sacrifice provided all of mankind with an everlasting covering for every bit of our sin. Christ's sacrifice was so perfect, so complete, so airtight, that God does not even see our sin anymore, only the perfect righteousness of the One who covers us. His atoning blood completely covers those who choose to take shelter under it. Have you?

Day Three

Cleansing Waters

From the first chapter of Genesis to the last chapter of John's Revelation, water is a theme throughout Scripture. The call for cleansing is a constant thread running through both the Old Testament and the New. God's desert sanctuary was no exception.

> With joy you will draw water from the wells of salvation.
>
> Isaiah 12:3

Outside the entrance to the Tabernacle stood a laver, or basin, of water. The Lord calls this laver a *kiyowr*. The Hebrew word is defined as something round, such as a washbowl, yet it also refers to a round *pulpit*. So what was God preaching to His Israelite congregation—and to us—from this bronze pulpit of water?

1. **Read Exodus 30:17-21. Describe the laver and its position.**

   _____

   _____

2. **According to the verses above, what were the priests required to do before ministering in the sanctuary? Under what penalty?**

   _____

   _____

3. **What are the measurements of the laver?** _____

   _____

4. **Read Ephesians 5:25-26, John 7:38-39, and Isaiah 12:3. What does water symbolize biblically?** _____

_____

5. **How might this relate to the laver's measurements?** _____

_____

_____

Just as with the golden lampstand, God provided no measurements for the laver that would cleanse the priests. With water symbolic of both God's Word and His Spirit, we are reminded that His Word is immeasurable and eternal, and the Holy Spirit is absolutely

> Your word, O Lord, is eternal.
> Psalm 119:89

uncontainable. If we attempt to serve God and man without the washing of His Word and the indwelling of His Spirit that comes with salvation, we, like uncleansed priests, will surely die for eternity.

> "The wind blows where it wishes and you hear the sound of it, but do not know where comes from and where it is going; so is everyone who is born of the Spirit."
> John 3:8 NAS

6. **Read Exodus 38:8. Where did the Israelites obtain the bronze to construct the laver?** _____

7. **What does this say about the hearts of the women?** _____

_____

_____

This basin wasn't just a hunk of bronze. God instructed the Israelites to fashion the laver out of the bronze mirrors used by the women who ministered at the Tent of Meeting. Mirrors! Whenever the

priests prepared to act on behalf of the people before God, they looked

at a reflection of their sinful selves against the backdrop of the

righteousness of God. The Lord commanded the priests to wash here

"that they die not."[39] Washing in these mirrors preserved the men's lives

by enabling them to put themselves and God in the true, proper

perspective.

8. **Read John 13:1-5,14-15. Share how this scene may relate to the Tabernacle laver.** _____

_____

_____

_____

On the eve of His crucifixion, Jesus took a basin, filled it with

water, and washed His friends' feet. God's

own Hand cleansed the disciples, preparing

them to minister as priests in His name.

Today, those who put their faith in Christ

become His priests. And as we wash in

God's Word and His Holy Spirit, we, too,

> You are a chosen race, a royal priesthood, a holy nation, God's own people, in order that you may proclaim the mighty acts of him who called you out of darkness into his marvelous light.
>
> I Peter 2:9 NRSV

are able—and called—to minister to the world in His name.

9. **Read Exodus 17:5-8 and Psalm 105:41. As they wandered in the desert in Zion, what was the source of the Israelites' water?**

_____

For forty years, the Israelites followed God in the parched desert,

> All of them drank the same miraculous water. For they all drank from the miraculous rock that traveled with them; and that rock was Christ.
>
> I Corinthians 10:4 NLT

yet were never themselves parched. God brought forth water from a rock to quench them and to cleanse them. A _rock_. In doing so, He pointed to the Rock of our salvation. The Christ who would one day become our source of Living Water.

Who would one day

> One of the soldiers pierced Jesus' side with a spear, bringing a sudden flow of blood and water.
>
> John 19:34

be struck that we might be cleansed and

drink freely the gift of life.

10. ✳ **Reflect on the following words from the classic hymn:**

Rock of ages cleft for me...Let the water and the blood, from Thy wounded side which flowed, be of sin the double cure, save from wrath and make me pure.

Augustus M. Toplady, 1776

_____
_____
_____
_____
_____

Day Four

The Place of Sacrifice

The focal point of the Lord's Old Testament House loomed in the court, gleaming in the desert sun. Here, upon the sacrificial altar, the penalty of sin was paid and reconciliation achieved for God's chosen ones day in and day out. This altar was as close to God as the eleven non-priestly tribes were permitted to come. And so, through their sacrifices, they communed here with their Lord through confession, sacrifice and worship.

> They built the altar of burnt offering of acacia wood.
>
> Exodus 38:1

1. **Read Exodus 27:1-8 and Numbers 4:5a,13-14. Describe the altar and its placement.** _____

    _____

2. **Recalling the symbolism we have already studied, describe the portrait that you see of Jesus in all of these materials.** _____

    _____
    _____
    _____
    _____

3. **What do you think the four horns may have symbolized?** ___

    _____
    _____

The acacia covered in bronze and purple was mirrored at Calvary,

when Jesus, the indestructible root from dry

ground, was mockingly robed in purple and led

to His own sacrifice. Yet both the Old

Testament altar and Christ's crucifiers pointed

perfectly to the end of time. For then the

> The soldiers made a crown of long, sharp thorns and put it on his head, and they put a royal purple robe on him.
>
> John 19:2 NLT

Father's sacrificial Son will return as the eternal King to judge all of

mankind.

The outward-pointing horns on the altar speak of the universal

nature of that future judgment—it will extend to the four corners of the

earth. But they also pointed to the universal nature of the *salvation*

> Repentance and forgiveness of sins will be preached in His name to all nations, beginning at Jerusalem.
>
> Luke 24:47

offered through Christ. For, while the sacrifices

laid upon the altar provided continual redemption

for the Israelites, the final sinless Sacrifice would

provide salvation for all mankind for all eternity.

4. **Read Leviticus 6:12-13. How often was the flame on the sacrificial altar to be lit?** _____

5. **Read Leviticus 9:24 and 2 Chronicles 7:1. What was the source of the fire that consumed the first offerings on behalf of the desert Israelites and the first offerings in Solomon's temple?**

_____

_____

6. **Reflect on what this says about God's role as initiator and Jesus' sacrifice.** _____

_____

_____

God Almighty lit that fire of forgiveness Himself, directly from Heaven. And the Initiator of that first sacrificial flame was again the

> "No one has taken [my life] away from me, but I lay it down on my own initiative."
>
> John 10:18 NAS

Initiator at the sacrificial altar of the Cross. No one could have placed Jesus on that altar against His will. Until that fateful day, during the years between Mount Sinai and Golgotha, the pleasing aroma of Jesus' future sacrifice continually ascended to the Father from the altar as He prepared a nation and a world to receive His Lamb.

7. **Read Exodus 29:38-43. What important aspect of the Lord's relationship with the Israelites is revealed here?** _____

_____

8. **Read Ephesians 3:11-12 and relate the Old Testament altar to the access to God that Jesus gives believers.** _____

_____

_____

For an ordinary Hebrew—one who could not enter the Tabernacle, perhaps the most precious piece of Scripture would be Exodus 29:43. For in that verse, God reveals where He would commune with the people. At that bronze altar, where the smell of flesh and fire continually filled the air, God met with His children. When they drew as

near to Him as they were permitted, that

In Him and through faith in Him we may approach God with freedom and confidence.

Ephesians 3:12

smell enveloped them with a keen awareness

of both their own sin and God's mercy and

grace.

So it is today. The Cross is where the eternal Lamb made the

ultimate sacrifice of grace and mercy on our behalf. And it is at the foot

of *that* altar where a person must meet God. It is the *only* place. When

we draw near, accepting the Sacrifice made on our behalf, we come face-

to-face with the Almighty. And, just like the Israelites who touched the

The altar shall be most holy, and whatever touches the altar shall be holy.

Exodus 29:37 NAS

altar, when we take up that sacrificial Cross, we

take on the holiness and righteousness of the

One who hung upon it.

Grab hold of the altar of the Lamb and be sanctified today!

Day Five

The Gateway to God

Over the past two weeks, we have encountered physical walls and objects that separated our Holy God from His unholy Beloved. Today, the layers become complete. You see, it wasn't enough that God had completely enshrouded the majestic sanctuary from view. He went further, commanding that a wall be erected around the Tabernacle, laver and altar. So not only were the Israelites prevented from looking inside the Tabernacle, they couldn't even come near it on their own accord—under penalty of death.

> "Anyone else [besides the priests] who approaches the sanctuary must be put to death."
>
> Numbers 3:10

1. **Read Exodus 38:16. Of what material were the courtyard walls made?** _____

2. **Recall the biblical symbolism of linen (see Week 2, Day 2) and reflect on the possible meanings of the wall for the Israelites.**
    _____
    _____
    _____

3. **Consider #2 and read John 1:14. Reflect on how the linen walls around God's earthly dwelling pointed to the future Messiah.**
    _____
    _____
    _____

The walls of the courtyard weren't made of majestic tapestries or bronze barriers. They were, instead, light, breezy linen. A reminder of the purity and righteousness of the One who resided within. And a prophetic picture of the human tent that would one day be filled with the full measure of God's perfection and righteousness: His only Begotten Son, the Messiah.

4. **Read Deuteronomy 29:29 and 1 Corinthians 2:9-10. Reflect on the possible message given by the height—7½ feet—of the linen wall.** _____

    _____

    _____

For those standing outside the Tabernacle court, it was impossible to view the things of God—the wall was simply too high.

> "When I tried to understand all this, it seemed hopeless until I entered God's sanctuary. Then I understood…
> Psalm 73:16-17
> HCSB

Even His earthly realm was a mystery to them. The truth is, none of us completely understands God's ways. But for those who stand inside His court—not inside the church walls, but inside God's Kingdom through faith in His Son—there is an insight into God's nature and heart that is impossible for an outside observer to grasp.

The reason has nothing to do with us, and everything to do with

God. For when we accept the Son into our

hearts, the Holy Spirit enters along with Him.

We are not left to fend for ourselves, but are

taught and encouraged by God Himself in the

Spirit.

> "But the Helper, the Holy Spirit, whom the Father will send in My name, He will teach you all things, and bring to your remembrance all that I said to you."
>
> John 14:26 NASB

But how could an ancient Israelite, physically separated from

God, catch a glimpse of Him?

5. **Read Leviticus 1:3,11; Leviticus 3:2; and Leviticus 4:4. What was the only circumstance under which the "lay" Israelites could enter the courtyard?** _____

    _____

6. **Read Exodus 38:18. Describe the courtyard gate.** _____
    _____
    _____

7. **Review the end of Day Two of last week and read John 14:6. What is the Messianic significance of this gate and the people's ability to enter in?** _____
    _____
    _____

While ordinary Israelites were not permitted to view the splendor

of God's Tabernacle, they were given a taste of it whenever they

presented a sacrifice. You see, in order to present an offering to God, an

Israelite had to walk through the courtyard gate. A gate that—just like the veil deep within the Tabernacle—depicted the majesty, righteousness, and suffering of the Messiah to come. As soon as the worshipper stepped inside that prophetic gate, he was ushered straight to the sacrificial altar, the place where God promised He would meet with the children of His flock.

Even though the ancient altar of sacrifice is gone today, the same

> "I am the gate; whoever enters through me will be saved."
> John 10:9

truth remains: In order to commune with our Holy God, we must first enter through the Messianic gate of Christ. And we, too, must bring a sacrifice. Not one of blood, but of faith. Faith in the Sacrifice already made on our behalf. When we take this step, we are ushered inside, able to discern what is true about God, ourselves, and the world around us. And we are able to personally unite with the Creator Himself.

> Your eyes will see the king in his beauty and view a land that stretches afar.
> Isaiah 33:17

8. ✳ **Have you entered God's sanctuary through the True Gate with your sacrifice of faith?** *If not,* **won't you pray to enter in today?** *If so,* **as part of God's royal priesthood, are you striving to usher others inside? Pray about how you might serve Him in this way.**

Week Four

The Great High Priest

> "But only the High Priest entered the inner room, and that only once a year, and never without blood, which he offered for himself and for the sins the people had committed in ignorance.
>
> Hebrews 9:7

Everything about the biblical High Priest was symbolic. His consecration ritual symbolized his complete dedication and obedience to God. His attire symbolized his representation of the nation, as well as the holiness of the Lord. And his one primary task—the Day of Atonement ritual—symbolized an offering up of the sinful lives of the people through the God-appointed substitute. Yet, the symbolism goes even deeper. These aspects of the High Priest were not only symbolic of the existing state of affairs, but they were a picture of what was yet to come—the Perfect High Priest, the Messiah, Jesus Himself.

We see this explicitly in the book of Hebrews. Many speculate that the author is Paul, formerly Saul, a Pharisee zealous for the law beyond compare. Whatever the author's identity, there is no mistaking that he understood the Law and treasured its fulfillment in Christ. In

Hebrews 4, this expert on the Law calls Jesus our Great High Priest,[40]

and in Hebrews 9 writes about the one time each year that the earthly

High Priest entered beyond the veil: the Day of Atonement. It was clear

to this Jewish scholar that Christ's atoning sacrifice on the Cross was the

perfect, divine fulfillment of the *Yom Kippur* ritual. As a result, it is

imperative that we, too, understand exactly who the High Priest was and

what he did.

For all the symbolism we will encounter, however, we must keep

in mind that Jesus was not a *reflection* of the Old Testament High Priest.

He was—and still is—the ultimate High Priest to which all before Him

pointed. Indeed, Jesus intercedes for us in the very Presence of God,

which was the ultimate function of the Old Testament High Priest. But

instead of interceding with the blood of goats and bulls, the Great High

Priest worked atonement with the most perfect blood of all: His own.

Day One

A Priest in the Line of... *Who?*

The Hebrew term for priest is *cohen*. It refers to a person who stands up for someone else, mediating for them in their situation.[h]   Prior to leading the Israelites through the Red Sea, the Lord established "household priests," commanding that every firstborn male be consecrated to Him. These men would offer sacrifices on behalf of their households. But

> "Consecrate to me every firstborn male. The first offspring of every womb among the Israelites belongs to me."
>
> Exodus 13:2

something happened shortly thereafter which led God to set apart only certain people to serve Him in His sanctuary.

1. **Read Exodus 32:19-29. Who did the Lord set apart and why?**
    _____
    _____
    _____

2. **Read Numbers 3:5-9. For what purpose did the Lord set the Levites apart?** _____

3. **Read Deuteronomy 14:28-29 and 26:12. How did the Levites support themselves and their families?** _____
    _____
    _____

---

[h] The definition of *cohen* explains why the word is used at times in Scripture to describe individuals who weren't God's anointed priests, but who represented people in other matters.

4. ✳ **Is there a path of service or decision to which God is currently calling you/your family that will require you to trust on Him for provision?** _____
_____
_____

As a result of the Levites' repentance and unquestioning commitment to Him, God appointed them to be the sole priestly class.[41] From that point on, Levite men served within the Tent of Meeting, and

> "My food," said Jesus, "is to do the will of Him who sent me and to finish His work."
>
> John 4:34

later the Temple. In Temple times, Levite women also had special roles in the community of faith, singing, playing instruments and composing sacred liturgical songs.[42] Supported by the people's tithes, those called to minister on God's behalf were not distracted from their primary task of serving God. Similarly, Jesus was sustained *by* His service, rather than *for* it.

But, while God set the Levites aside to be His priestly *class*, not all Levites were actual *priests*.

5. **Read Numbers 18:1-7. Within the tribe of Levi, who were to be the priests?** _____

6. **Read Exodus 28:1-2. Who was the first High Priest?** _____

7. **Read Exodus 29:29 and Numbers 20:24-28. How was the High Priest determined going forward from Aaron?** _____
_____

Moses and Aaron were themselves Levites. Perhaps that is why it was their tribe that rallied to God after the Golden Calf fiasco. And, graciously redeeming Aaron from his role in that sin, God allowed him to become the first High Priest. The office would continue to pass down to the eldest son in Aaron's line throughout the generations,[43] with Aaron's other descendants serving as the supporting priests, and the rest of the Levites serving as the priests' assistants. These distinctions speak once more to the theme of separations ordained between God and His people.

But what about Jesus? What is our Great High Priest's lineage?

8. **Read Matthew 1:1-16. Keeping in mind that the sons of Jacob (also called "Israel") were the heads of each of the twelve tribes, from which tribe was Jesus descended? Did He belong to the earthly priesthood?** _____

9. **Read Psalm 110:4 and Hebrews 6:20. From what biblical priesthood did Jesus derive His authority?** _____
   _____

10. **Read Genesis 14:18-20. What do we learn about Melchizedek?**
    _____
    _____
    _____
    _____

11. **Did Melchizedek minister to Abraham before or after God made His covenant with Abram/Abraham?** _____

12. **Read Hebrews 7:1-3. What are the meanings of Melchizedek's name?** _____

_____

13. **Read Isaiah 43:13, 49:6 and Ephesians 2:14. What do these verses about the Messiah and the above facts about Melchizedek say about the type of priest Jesus was to be, and about the scope of His ministry?** _____

_____

_____

_____

_____

_____

By prophesying that the Messiah would be in the order of Melchizedek, David spoke volumes about the future Savior. He would be a righteous King of Peace (*"Salem"*) who would also mediate for us before God. With no record of Melchizedek's birth or death in all of Scripture, a priest in his order would have no end and no beginning. Finally, because Melchizedek served Abram before his covenant with God, a priest in Melchizedek's order would intercede on behalf of all mankind, not just God's covenant people, Israel. Indeed, Jesus is our eternal, righteous King of Peace who offered His sacrifice on behalf of all mankind for all time.

> And His name shall be called... Prince of Peace.
> Isaiah 9:6
> KJV

> God was reconciling the world to Himself in Christ.
> 2 Cor. 5:19

Day Two

A Man Without Blemish

Because the High Priest would actually enter God's Presence,

there were strict physical requirements for the men who occupied this

office. These requirements could not, of course, make the High Priest

truly perfect, but they symbolized the purity and holiness required in

God's Presence. Further, the requirements

pointed to the perfect, sinless High Priest yet to

come. While the external requirements set forth

in Scripture were numerous and specific

(including even the length of hair), four stand out

in particular.

> Every high priest is selected from among men and is appointed to represent them in matters related to God...
>
> Hebrews 5:1

1. **Read Leviticus 21:16-23. Reflect on the physical perfection required by God of His priests.** _____
    _____
    _____
    _____

Any physical imperfection rendered a descendant of Aaron

unable to conduct the priestly duties of sacrifice. To do so would

"profane" God's sanctuary. This is a key point, because while we routinely speak of the perfection of Christ as the sacrifice, we often

overlook the command that the *offeror* was to be

without blemish as well. On Calvary, our perfect

Sacrifice for sin was offered up by One who was,

Himself, without defect as well—including the

defect of sin, which plagued even the most

physically perfect High Priest.

> For the Law
> appoints as high
> priests men who
> are weak; but the
> oath...appointed
> the Son, who has
> been made
> perfect forever.
> Hebrews 7:28

2. **Read Leviticus 21:7,13-15. Reflect on the fact that Jesus, the
    Great High Priest, has chosen the Church as His Bride.** ____

    _____

    _____

    _____

Marrying anyone besides a virgin would profane and pollute the

priestly line. In the same way, God could not be joined to you or me in

our natural state of sinfulness. So did He go and

find another bride? No, He loved you too much

to leave you. So He cleansed you Himself,

purifying you with His own Blood, that He might

be joined to you for eternity.

> "For your
> Maker is your
> husband... the
> Holy One of
> Israel is your
> Redeemer."
> Isaiah 54:5

3. **In Leviticus 21:12, what did the Lord forbid the High Priest
    from doing?** _____

4. **Relate this to Jesus, our Great High Priest.** _____

_____

_____

_____

While other priests could come and go freely, the High Priest was

forbidden from ever leaving the sanctuary. While Jesus did leave the

sanctuary of Heaven to be with us, He never left the sanctuary of God's

> For in Christ all
> the fullness of the
> Deity lives in
> bodily form.
>
> Colossians 2:9

Presence, for God dwelled within Him. Jesus was,

Himself, God "simply" wrapped in flesh.

Anywhere Jesus roamed was God's sanctuary,

whether He was teaching seekers in the Temple court or healing

demoniacs in the graveyard.

5. **Read Leviticus 21:1-4, Numbers 19:11-13, and Luke 10:30-37. In all likelihood, why did the priest and the Levite pass by the dying man in the road between Jericho and Jerusalem?**

_____

_____

6. **Compare Leviticus 21:1-2 with 21:10-11. What was the difference between the rules concerning dead bodies for the High Priest and the other priests?** _____

_____

_____

7. **Read Numbers 9:5-11, John 19:38-42, and Mark 16:1-7,. What does the corpse prohibition say about these New Testament individuals' commitment to and love for Jesus?** _____

_____

_____

_____

The High Priest could not so much as enter a room containing a

dead body—even if it was one of his parents! For a priest or Levite

> "Whoever
> touches the
> dead body of
> anyone will
> be unclean for
> seven days."
>
> Numbers
> 19:11

traveling *to* Jerusalem to minister in the Temple, or on

his way *back* to Jericho to share about his incredible

experience there, touching a man near death would

seriously hinder his once-in-a-lifetime opportunity. So

the men remained ceremonially clean, yet morally

defiled by leaving a fellow man to perish.

8. **Read Luke 7:11-15, 8:49-56 and John 11:38-44. How can you
    reconcile Jesus' perfect obedience to the Law with His
    interaction with the dead?** _____

    _____

    _____

Just like the earthly High Priests, Jesus simply could not tolerate

proximity to death. Yet rather than avoiding it, Jesus conquered death by

raising the dead back to life. In His *own* tomb, Jesus could not even be in

the presence of His own dead body.

Rather, in the midst of His own death, He

lived, banishing death forever!

> "...Why do you look
> for the living among the
> dead? He is not here;
> He has risen!"
>
> Luke 24:5-6

Day Three

Clothed in Godliness

We have learned that a man's lineage and physical condition

determined his acceptability as the Lord's Old Testament High Priest.

The garments he wore served as an outward reminder

of this distinction. While all priests wore four sacred

vestments (linen breeches, coat, girdle, and head

covering), God designed an additional four sacred

items for the High Priest to wear. All adorned with

gold, the "golden vestments" clearly differentiated

this man from the other priests.[44]

> "Make sacred garments for your brother Aaron, to give him dignity and honor."
>
> Exodus 28:2

1. **Read Exodus 28:6-14. Describe the High Priest's *ephod*, or vest.**
   _____
   _____

2. **Read Exodus 28:15-30. Briefly describe the breastplate.**
   _____
   _____

3. **What purpose did it serve?** _____
   _____

4. **Read Isaiah 53:12 and 1 Peter 2:24. Compare the role of the shoulder pieces and breastplate to Jesus' work as our Great High Priest.** _____
   _____

_____

_____

On his shoulders and across his chest, the High Priest bore the names of the twelve tribes of Israel. They served as a constant reminder

> Praise to the Lord, to God our Savior, who daily bears our burdens.
>
> Psalm 68:19

that his job was to serve and represent his people before God. And as the High Priest ministered before the Lord, the engraved stones "reminded" the Lord of His people. As if He could forget.

As Jesus walked the earth, the divine High Priest carried His children not with symbolic jewels over His chest, but inside His very heart, making every decision with perfect love and discernment on behalf of each child He created. Then, on the Cross, Jesus bore the sins not only of Israel but of every tongue and tribe in all creation. And this He did not through symbolic garments, but in His very flesh.

5. **Compare the symbolism of the jewels in Exodus 28:17-21 and in Revelation 21:14,19-20.** _____

   _____

   _____

The precious gems carried over the heart of the High Priest represented the twelve tribes of Israel. God will surely honor His Chosen in the New Jerusalem. But the city will be built upon the foundation of the twelve who first proclaimed His Son, the Messiah, to Israel and to the world.

6. **Read Exodus 28:31-35. Briefly describe the High Priest's robe, the *meil*, which he wore beneath the ephod.** _____

_____

The 76 (by tradition) bells alternating with the pomegranates on the High Priest's robe announced his presence in the Holy Place, averting death. On *Yom Kippur*, however, the bells would be left behind when he entered the *Most* Holy Place, adorned only in linen (see Week 5, Day 1).

7. **Read Leviticus 21:10 and John 19:23-24. Compare the High Priest's robe with the clothes Jesus wore as He performed His last High Priestly duty.** _____

_____
_____

God commanded that the seamless *meil* never be torn, and that it be promptly removed as soon as the High Priest's ministerial duties were finished.[45] As soon as Jesus completed His ministry, as soon as He had provided atonement for all mankind with His own blood, His garment was taken from Him. His job was finished. And, true to

> They divide my garments among them and cast lots for my clothing.
>
> Psalm 22:18

both God's command and David's prophecy, the Roman soldiers at the Cross cast lots rather than tear Christ's perfect, priestly garment.

Finally, the High Priest wore a turban, different from the

headbands (v.40) worn by the other priests. But what truly set the High

Priest's turban apart was the golden plate attached to it.

8. **Read Exodus 28:36-38. What was written on the golden plate secured to the High Priest's linen turban?** _____

9. **What was its function?** _____
    _____

10. **Read Matthew 8:17. Compare Jesus with the function of the plate.** _____
    _____
    _____

Even our sacred gifts to the Lord are tainted with sin! Whether

it's wrong motivation or unconfessed sin, our gifts to and efforts for God

are covered in guilt. Thankfully our sinful mind is covered by the perfect

Head of Christ, thoroughly dedicated to God's holy purposes. What a

blessing! Jesus' sacrifice not only frees us from condemnation, it actually

allows us to give freely back to our Lord and our Savior in spite of

ourselves!

11. **✳ As a priest of the New Covenant, how would your thoughts and walk be different if "Holy to the Lord" was tangibly written upon your forehead for all to see?** _____
    _____
    _____
    _____

Day Four

Consecration

Before assuming his office, the High Priest was consecrated to his ministry. The elaborate and detailed ceremony included three anointings: one of water, one of oil, and one of blood. Each of these anointings is also found in the course of Jesus' ministry as our Great High Priest.

> Those were the names of Aaron's sons, the anointed priests, who were ordained to serve as priests.
>
> Numbers 3:3

1. **Read Leviticus 8:5-6. What was the first step of the High Priest consecration?** _____

2. **Read Luke 3:21-23. What was the first step in Jesus' active ministry?** _____

Just as with the earthly High Priest, Jesus' baptism consecrated the beginning of His earthly ministry. And what a benediction He

> As Jesus was coming up out of the water, he saw heaven being torn open...And a voice came from heaven: "You are my Son, whom I love; with you I am well pleased."
>
> Mark 1:10-11

received—the Voice of the Almighty booming through the split-open heavens! Jesus did not, however, experience the next two anointings until the eve and completion of His sacrifice. We shall soon see why.

3. After the ceremonial washing with water, the High Priest donned his sacred garments, and then received the anointing of oil. Read Exodus 30:22-33. Describe the anointing oil. ____

_____

_____

_____

4. Read John (a) 12:1-8, (b) John 19:38-42, and (c) Luke 22:39-46. How were these ingredients of the sacred priestly anointing oil reflected in Jesus' last days and burial?

   a. Perfume _____

   _____

   b. Myrrh _____

   _____

   c. Olive Oil _____

   _____

The night before Jesus' triumphal entry into Jerusalem, Mary anointed Him with perfume, just as the High Priest was anointed with

> He poured some of the anointing oil on Aaron's head and anointed him to consecrate him.
> Leviticus 8:12

fragrant spices. Then, on the eve of His crucifixion, Jesus prayed in agony in the Garden of Gethsemane—literally the Garden of the Olive Press. Just as olives were crushed for their precious

oil, our precious Savior was crushed in spirit at the thought of His task at hand. Finally, when Joseph of Arimethea and Nicodemus took Jesus' lifeless body from the Cross, they brought with them a

> "She poured perfume on my body beforehand to prepare for my burial."
> Mark 14:8

75-pound mixture of myrrh and aloes, preparing Him for burial—and anointing Him to His next task: resurrection. Jesus' high priestly anointment was perfect, fulfilling even these small details.

5. **Read Leviticus 8:22-23. Describe the blood anointing of the High Priest consecration ritual and the symbolism you personally find in it.** _____

_____

_____

_____

_____

The right ear, thumb and toe. Listen, serve, and follow. In everything Jesus did, He served and honored the Father in His receptiveness to those around Him, His gentle and healing touch, and in

> "I love the Father and...I do exactly what my Father has commanded me."
>
> John 14:31

His purposeful and obedient steps. Even to the mount of Calvary. Jesus' heavenly anointment was clearly marked by His steadfast commitment to God's eternal plan, and by His perfect, divine ability to achieve it.

6. **Read Matthew 8:28-32, Mark 4:39, Mark 10:46-52, Luke 23:34 and skim John 17. What difference in authority do you notice between Jesus' words before and after the Last Supper?** ____

_____

_____

_____

7. **When, therefore, do you think did Jesus stepped from His role as divine Commander into His role as the divine Intercessor?**

_____

_____

During His ministry, Jesus healed sickness and forgave sins on His own authority. Yes, He prayed to the Father about these things, but

> "All authority in heaven and on earth has been given to me."
> Matthew 28:18

Jesus was the One who offered healing, condemned demons, and silenced the sea. Jesus was not the intermediary, He was the One.

But then, at the Last Supper, on the eve of His own sacrifice, we see Jesus' transformation. He interceded on behalf of all believers in the Upper Room. And from the Cross, Jesus did not bestow forgiveness from Himself. Instead, He petitioned the Father to forgive us—all of us who by our sin placed Him upon that tree. Jesus had become the Intercessor, the Highest Priest, making intercession and presenting the perfect atoning sacrifice for all mankind.

Day Five

Still Just a Man

For all the outward splendor and physical perfection that marked

the High Priest of Israel, there was to

be no mistaking that he was just as

human as the rest of his brethren.

> There is not a righteous
> man on earth who does
> what is right and never sins.
> Ecclesiastes 7:20

1. **Read Leviticus 16:11. What type of offering did the High Priest make at the onset of the *Yom Kippur* ritual? On whose behalf?**

    _____

2. **What did this communicate to the High Priest and to the congregation?** _____

    _____

3. **Read Leviticus 4:3-7 and 16:14. Where did God require the High Priest to bring the blood of his sin offering on that day, as opposed to other times he brought his own sin offerings to the Lord?** _____

    _____

The fact that God required the High Priest to first make

atonement for himself was a strong reminder that this man's role was

purely symbolic. There was to be no mistaking the fact that, despite his

holy status, the High Priest was just as sinful as other men. And, in order

to cleanse others, the High Priest had to first be cleansed of his own sin.

The most powerful aspect of the High Priest's sin offering is the fact

that, on this most holy day, he had to bring

his perfect blood cover to the mercy seat—

the very Throne of God. Can you imagine

taking that step into the Holy of Holies—

alone, in the smoky stillness, stripped of your

> Do not think of
> yourself more highly
> than you ought, but
> rather think of yourself
> with sober judgment,
> in accordance with the
> measure of faith God
> has given you.
> Romans 12:3

golden robes,[i] to atone for your *personal* sins before the earthly Throne of

the Most High God? How unbelievably humbling.

In stark contrast to the high priestly ritual, Jesus, our perfect High

Priest, did not have to present a sin offering for Himself before making

atonement for the nation of humanity, because He was entirely without

sin. Christ's sacrifice on the final Day of Atonement was not *for* Himself,

only *of* Himself.

4. **Read Luke 2:22-24. What was the only sacrifice offered in connection with Jesus' life that is ever recorded in Scripture?**
_____
_____

5. **Read Leviticus 12:6-8. What type of offerings did Mary and Joseph present? On whose behalf?** _____
_____
_____

---

[i] See Week 5, Day 2.

6. **Read Numbers 3:50-51. What was involved in consecrating Mary and Joseph's firstborn to the Lord?** _____

_____

_____

It was Mary's sin they atoned for on Jesus' first day in the Temple—her sin of simply being a mortal mother, unclean from childbirth. The priest accepted Mary's offering, declaring her clean following her forty days of purification. It is astounding to know that three decades later, Mary's son would sacrifice Himself to cleanse her forever.

There was no need to purify the sinless Christ child on His first mortal day in the Temple. Instead, in those beautiful moments, Jesus' life was formally dedicated to His Father. Mary and Joseph acknowledged, in a way no other parents could, that their son was not their own—He truly belonged to the Heavenly Father. On that incredible day, our Jesus was redeemed from God by His earthly family, so that one day He might redeem them. Can you imagine their thoughts that day?

7. ✳ **Meditate on the following verses, reflecting on your own sin, and praising God for the perfection of your Great High Priest, Jesus His Son, who intercedes on your behalf.**

Who can say, "I have kept my heart pure;
I am clean and without sin"?
Proverbs 20:9

"He is the Rock, his works are perfect, and all his ways are just.
A faithful God who does no wrong, upright and just is he."
Deuteronomy 32:4

All of us have become like one who is unclean,
and all our righteous acts are like filthy rags.
Isaiah 64:6

For we do not have a high priest who is unable to sympathize
with our weaknesses, but we have one who has been tempted in every way,
just as we are—yet was without sin.
Hebrews 4:15

Forgiven and purified, the earthly High Priest emerged from the

veil. He was ready to reenter that Most Holy Place once more, so that

the rest of the nation might join him in his state of peace with the Most

Holy God. Here, at the edge of national atonement, the purified High

Priest pointed straight ahead to the Great High Priest to come. The One

in the order of Melchizedek. The One who had no need of a perfect

blood cover, because perfect blood coursed through His veins.

The perfect Offeror was about to become the perfect Offering.

Week Five

The Ritual Begins

A voice of one calling: "In the desert prepare the way for the
Lord; make straight in the wilderness a highway for our God."

Isaiah 40:3

So many times in life, the preparation for a big event is more
time-consuming, more crucial, more life-changing than the actual event
itself. While the Day of Atonement's blood ritual was of unparalleled
importance to God's people, the path leading to the sacrificial altar was
profound as well. And so, this week, we will consider the steps of the
High Priest as he approached the atonement sacrifice. And we will
discover how they were paralleled in the steps of Jesus as the Messiah
strode to the edge of His own Sacrifice.

During Temple times, the High Priest ate a small meal on the eve
of *Yom Kippur*.[46] He then received instruction from the Sanhedrin elders
on the procedure and meaning of the atonement ritual he was about to
conduct. They wanted to be sure that nothing was taken for granted.

These select few fellowshipped with the High Priest through the entire night, keeping him awake to focus on his task at hand.

For the Messiah, the evening before His atonement sacrifice was remarkably similar, yet turned completely around. Jesus, too, broke bread with a small group of supporters. Yet their meal wasn't scant, for they celebrated the Feast of Unleavened Bread with the Bread of Life Himself. And, instead of *receiving* teaching, the Great High Priest was—as always—teaching others, praying for them, and sharing His last hours His friends, so that nothing was taken for granted.

Unfortunately, the select few chosen to keep Jesus awake that night literally fell asleep on the job, while the Messiah communed in anguish with God until daybreak.

No matter. He was ready. After all, He'd had this moment in mind since the beginning of time.

Day One

Immersed

Ceremonial cleanliness is a major theme of Leviticus; the words 'clean' and 'unclean' are used 46 and 123 times, respectively. The ceremonial cleansing process always involved a washing with water, and the *Yom Kippur* ritual of Leviticus 16 was no exception. Before beginning the annual atonement ritual, the High Priest was commanded to bathe.[i]

> "These are sacred garments; so he must bathe himself with water before he puts them on."
>
> Leviticus 16:4

1. **What do you think bathing before the atonement ritual symbolized?** _____

_____

The High Priest was not the only one who immersed himself on the Day of Atonement. Some Jews then and even now immerse themselves prior to the commencement of *Yom Kippur*, sharing in the reverent preparation for the ritual.[47] Similarly, a multitude of people sought ritual cleansing at the beginning of Jesus' ministry as well.

---

[i] During Temple times, the High Priest immersed himself five times, and washed his hands and feet ten times, during the course of performing the daily offerings and the atonement ritual on *Yom Kippur* [Bloch (1978), Edersheim (1994) and Hall (2004)].

2. **Read Matthew 3:11, Mark 1:4, and Acts 19:4. What was the purpose of John's baptism?** _____

_____

3. **Read Matthew 3:13-16. Jesus was without sin, yet He underwent John's baptism. Why?** _____

_____

_____

_____

_____

Personal repentance is a prerequisite to salvation. The atoning blood of Christ will not provide cover for someone who refuses to acknowledge and repent of their sinful nature. John's baptism, and the

> This water symbolizes baptism that now saves you also—not the removal of dirt from the body but the pledge of a good conscience toward God. It saves you by the resurrection of Jesus Christ.
>
> I Peter 3:21

High Priest's *Yom Kippur* immersion, symbolized the repentance of someone prepared to receive the true spiritual cleansing yet to come.

In contrast, Jesus' own baptism was not one of repentance, for He was without sin. But it did demonstrate the nature of Jesus' submission to God, and His determination to walk the same steps as the people He had come to shepherd into "all righteousness."[48] And, just as the High Priest began his annual atonement ministry with immersion, Jesus' baptism marked the beginning of His long, determined march to the eternally-atoning Cross.

Let's wade together into these waters a bit further, because the Old Testament immersion waters tie directly into the words and identity of the coming Christ.

4. **Read Leviticus 11:36a, Leviticus 15:13, and 2 Kings 5:10-14. Describe the nature of water used to make someone ceremonially clean.** _____
_____

5. **Consider this in the context of Jesus' words in John 4:10 and 7:38.** _____
_____
_____
_____

The water used for immersion—both for priests and for everyday Jews—had to be pure. It couldn't be drawn and held in a vessel, it must, instead, be "living" water, found at its natural source. When Jesus called

> "And he shall wash his flesh in living water and be clean."
> Leviticus 15:13
> DRV

> "He who believes in Me... from his innermost being will flow rivers of living water."
> John 7:38

Himself Living Water, then, it meant something very significant to the Jews of His day: pure, living water provided spiritual cleansing for their souls, not just quenching for their thirst.

The living water in which the priests bathed, flowed beneath the Temple in the very aqueduct constructed by Hezekiah in 702 B.C.[49] Not

only did this immersion
water supply the priestly
bathing rooms, but they also
fed the Pool of Siloam.

> As for the...pool and the tunnel by which [Hezekiah] brought water into the city, are they not written in the book of the annals of the kings of Judah?
> 2 Kings 20:20

6. **Read John 9:1-12 and reflect on the significance of Jesus' healing command in light of what we have learned.** _____
   _____
   _____

7. **Read Jeremiah 2:13 and 17:13. What further significance is there in Jesus calling Himself the Living Water?** _____
   _____

By calling Himself "Living Water," Jesus not only claimed to be the source of spiritual cleansing, but He also declared His *deity*. The earthly High Priest, as we well know, was *not* deity. And so he allowed the living waters of the Temple to wash over him, preparing his heart to

> "...the water I'll give him will be in him a spring of water bubbling up to everlasting life."
> John 4:10b
> BECK

offer the blood substitute for himself and for his people. Centuries later, as the Christ climbed the hill to the Cross, He had no need for personal, ceremonial cleansing that day. For He has been the source of Living Water since the beginning of time, now being poured out to cleanse us all.

Drench yourself in His mercy today.

Day Two

Stripped

To bathe, which we studied yesterday, the High Priest obviously had to remove his clothing. But when the cleansed man then dressed in preparation for the atonement ritual, he donned a simple linen tunic. On this most sacred day of the year, the pinnacle of his priestly responsibilities, the High Priest was humbled, stripped of his gold and jewels. He would work atonement in the Presence of God, conscious all the while that before the Almighty, he wasn't golden, but completely transparent.

> "He is to put on the sacred linen tunic, with linen undergarments next to his body; he is to tie the linen sash around him and put on the linen turban."
> Leviticus 16:4

1. **Read Luke 2:7, 2 Corinthians 8:9, and Philippians 2:7-8. Reflect on these verses, considering the tangible things Jesus was willing to give up in order to present His atoning sacrifice.**
    _____
    _____
    _____

2. **Read Colossians 1:16, Matthew 20:28, and Zechariah 9:9. Recalling the symbolism of linen (purity, righteousness, humility), reflect on the contrast between Christ's true supremacy and the attitude toward Himself and others He demonstrated while on earth.** _____
    _____

_____

_____

_____

3. **Read Matthew 4:1-11, Luke 20:20-26, and 1 Peter 2:23. Jesus was tempted by Satan and provoked by the self-righteous. Yet what was the nature of His response to and interaction with others? Why?** _____

_____

_____

Jesus exchanged His garments of glory and majesty for those of poverty and humility. Just becoming a human being was a humbling enough move, let alone waking up as a poor naked infant, breathing in the stench of a stable. But Jesus went further than that. Not only did He give

> "...I am gentle and humble in heart."
> Matthew 11:29

up the glory of heaven for our sakes, but He lived a life stripped of any semblance of outward importance or superiority.

As He embarked upon His ministry to shepherd and save God's children, Jesus answered trickery with Truth and entrapment with enlightenment. He never pulled the King of Creation card. And He

> "...He shall be called: The Lord our Righteousness."
> Jeremiah 23:6 KJV

never reacted out of prideful anger or defensiveness. Jesus was never about Himself, but always about the Father.

Yet Jesus' stripping went beyond His choice to put off His

heavenly majesty in exchange for human flesh. His stripping went

beyond His attitude of humility and His never-

ending righteousness. No, on the last day of

Jesus' mortal life, He endured the worst

possible stripping we could imagine.

> When Jesus entered Jerusalem, the whole city was stirred and asked, "Who is this?"
> Matthew 21:10

4. **Read Deuteronomy 16:16-17 and John 12:12. What do these verses mean for the population of Jerusalem during Jesus' trial and crucifixion?** _____

   _____

5. ✳ **Read Matthew 27:26-35, Mark 15:15-32, and Luke 23:34. Meditate on the pain and humiliation that the Prince of Peace endured.** _____

   _____
   _____
   _____

6. ✳ **Pray your thoughts about this to the Lord.**

As Jesus presented His perfect sacrifice that final Day of

Atonement, He allowed Himself to be stripped naked by mockers,

enduring the worst kind of humiliation and torture. Even while He hung

dying on the Cross, Jesus watched soldiers draw straws to steal His

modest clothing. And all of this happened in the midst of a Jerusalem swelling with more than 600,000 families who had journeyed to observe

the Passover.[50]

7. ✻ **Have you ever experienced the public pain of ridicule, or the physical and emotional pain of assault? If so, have you allowed Jesus to heal your heart? He wants to, and He can, because He's been there, too.** _____

_____

_____

_____

_____

_____

_____

On *Yom Kippur*, the High Priest was stripped of his majestic

garments for a few hours at most. When Jesus came to offer our

atonement sacrifice—Himself—He shed the very majesty and authority

of heaven to indwell the decaying body of a helpless human child. The

Lord of all lived a life of service and humility. And His earthly reward

was nothing but agonizing torture, public humiliation, and an

excruciating death. Why did He endure it? Simply because He loves you

deeply, and was committed to rescue you and clothe you with His grace

and mercy for all eternity.

> We don't have a priest who is out of touch with our reality. He's been through weakness and testing, experienced it all - all but the sin.
> Hebrews 4:15, The Message

Day Three

A Lamb Without Blemish

Cleansed and then clothed in humility, the High Priest emerged, prepared to offer the national atonement sacrifice. He stepped to the gate of the Tent of Meeting, ready to take hold of the sacrificial lambs. In God's perfect plan, the day on which Jesus made His triumphal entry into Jerusalem was "lamb selection day."[51] On this day, the Jews who flocked to Jerusalem chose the Passover lambs they would offer on behalf of their family. And so, as both the High Priest and Jesus approached their people, the perfect atonement lambs were selected. But only one Lamb's blood would last for eternity.

> "From the Israelite community he is to take two male goats for a sin offering..."
>
> Leviticus 16:5

1. **Read Leviticus 16:5. What type of animal was to be the *Yom Kippur* atonement offering?** _____

2. **Read Leviticus 9:15, 22-24. What animal was offered as the first sacrifice on behalf of the nation of Israel?** _____

Most people associate lambs with sheep. But in Exodus 12:5, we learn that God allowed sacrificial "lambs" to be taken from either the sheep or the goats. Goats, the animals specified for *Yom Kippur* and for individual sin offerings, were known for their strong unpleasant odor.[52]

And so, as the community presented them to the High Priest, they were

confronted with the stench of their sin.

At the same time, they could also be reminded of the very first sin

sacrifice and be assured of their covenant with God: That first national

sin offering in Leviticus 9 was actually the *first* act of the *first* High Priest

...the Lamb that
was slain from
the foundation
of the world.
Revelation
13:8b

under God's covenant with Israel. One day, on the

final Day of Atonement, the perfect High Priest

would offer the Lamb whose Sacrifice was ordained

from the beginning of time. The sin sacrifice that

would mark the first day of God's new covenant with all of humanity.

3. **Read Leviticus 4:13-14. On occasions other than the Day of
    Atonement, what animal was to be used for the national sin
    offering?** _____

4. **Read Leviticus 5:5-6. What was to be used as the sin offering of
    individual members of the community?** _____

5. **Why do you think that the animal typically presented as an
    individual sin offering was used as the corporate sin offering on
    Yom Kippur?** _____

    _____

    _____

    _____

    _____

    _____

With the exception of *Yom Kippur*, bulls served as community sin offerings, while goats served as personal sin offerings. By commanding the use of goats for *Yom Kippur*, God made it clear that the national sin ritual was applicable to each member of the nation of Israel. In the same way, Jesus made His universal sacrifice for each and every person, therefore requiring a personal response.

6. **Read Exodus 12:5 and Leviticus 22:19-21. Why do you suppose sacrificial lambs could not be younger than one year?** _____
   _____
   _____
   _____

7. **Read Luke 2:52 and 23:4. How do these verses speak to Jesus as a fitting blood sacrifice?** _____
   _____
   _____
   _____

Tamiym is the Hebrew word used to describe the perfection of suitable sacrifices; it means perfect, or wholly-sound. The word is used to describe not only fitting sacrifices or upright believers, but the Lord Himself and His perfect Word. God demanded a perfect sacrifice of body and soul. To determine such perfection, a subject must be observed over a period of time—a lamb younger than one year had not yet proved itself. Was it

> As for God, His way is perfect.
> Psalm 18:30a

physically sound? How did it respond to the daily tests of life? As Jesus

grew, He found increasing favor with God and man. Others observed

Jesus and deemed Him to be without sin—even those who opposed

Him. In fact, the very man who sentenced

> "I find no basis for a charge against him."
> John 19:4b

Jesus to death could find no fault with Him!

Jesus was, indeed, fitting for—though not deserving of—sacrifice.

8. **Re-read Leviticus 16:5. Who provided the sacrificial lambs for the *Yom Kippur* atonement ritual?** _____

9. **Who provided the offering for our final, eternal atoning sacrifice? How did this fundamentally change the nature of atonement for mankind?** _____

_____

_____

Year after year, the sons of Israel provided from their own

possessions the perfect sacrificial lamb for the annual atonement ritual.

In contrast, at the Cross, God Himself provided the Substitute. Just as

He had done for Abraham, when He spared the

life of Abraham's son, Isaac. But this time, the

Son was not spared. This time, on the final day

> "God Himself will provide the lamb for the burnt offering, my son."
> Genesis 22:8

of substitutionary atonement, the *Son* was the provision, and we were the

ones spared. The Most High God selected and provided His perfect

Child in exchange for His children, once and for all.

Day Four

"You Cannot Come"

On the Day of Atonement, when the Israelites presented their

sacrificial lambs to the High Priest, they relinquished all control. They

understood that what this man was about to

do, he must do alone. Even though these

most sacred moments impacted all of God's

people, the atonement ritual itself was entirely

between the High Priest and the Lord. No

one, not even another priest, was permitted to

even enter the Tent of Meeting during the

ritual.

> "No one is to be in the Tent of Meeting from the time Aaron goes in to make atonement in the Most Holy Place until he comes out, having made atonement for himself, his household, and the whole community of Israel."
>
> Leviticus 16:17

1. **Read John 7:33 and 16:32. Reflect on the solitude of the High Priest's task and how it parallels the way Jesus saves us.** ____

   _____

   _____

   _____

   _____

2. **Read Galatians 2:15-16, Ephesians 2:8-9, and 2 Timothy 1:9. What do these verses say about your role in the salvation process?** _____

   _____

   _____

Throughout the year, the Israelites participated in their own sin offerings. They presented their lambs to the priest, slaughtered them with their own hands, and looked on as the priest flayed and arranged the sacrifices on the altar. But not on *Yom Kippur*. On this day, they gave up control, trusting their fate to God's High Priest.

On Calvary, Jesus entered a place that no one else could go. He entered death, not to submit to it, but to conquer it forever. Jesus entered death with His own Divine blood, to purchase the pardon none

> Where I am
> going you cannot
> come."
> John 13:33b

of us could afford. Every day since then, mankind has been instructed to simply trust in that work. In order to receive our eternal pardon, we are commanded to let go and allow the Messiah to save us. To trust in the sacrifices of our own hands would be a deadly mistake.

3. **Read Numbers 3:10 and John 13:36. What is the key difference between the people's ability to follow the High Priest into God's Presence in the Old Testament, and our ability to follow Jesus there now?** _____

_____

_____

_____

_____

_____

After the completion of the atonement ritual, the priests were permitted to reenter the sanctuary, but the rest of the Israelites were, still, forbidden. Despite the atoning sacrifice made in God's very Presence, the layers of separation between Him and His people remained. They were forgiven, but still unclean.

> ...again and again [the priest] offers the same sacrifices, which can never take away sins.
>
> Hebrews 10:11

In stark contrast, after Jesus' perfect sacrifice on the Cross, not only were His disciples—His priests, if you will—allowed to follow Him into God's Presence, but everyone else was invited as well. Including you and me. The blood of the Lamb has covered the sin that separated us from our Most Holy Lord. Isn't it *incredible*? Once we accept that we

> "...you cannot follow now, but you will follow later."
>
> John 13:36b

cannot enter God's Presence through our own efforts, we are invited to go to the very place that seemed so inaccessible!

4. **Consider the following verses: Ephesians 3:12, Romans 5:1-2 and 6:8, Matthew 4:19 and 7:21, John 14:2 and 21:18-19, 1 Peter 2:21-23, 1 John 1:7, and Hebrews 12:9.**

    We know we are invited to follow Christ, but where is it that He leads us? On the next page, circle where believers are called to follow Jesus and cross out ones to which we are specifically called not to go.

Suffering	Perfect health	Retaliation
Happiness	Physical death	Sin
Peace	Heaven	Holiness
God's Presence	Obedience	Material comfort
Christian fellowship	Eternal life	Humility
Earthly success	Evangelism	Outward piety

5. ✳ **Where are you willing to follow Him?** _____
   _____
   _____

6. ✳ **Are you hesitating to follow Him somewhere that He is inviting you to come? Or are you lingering in a place He has not called you to be? Where and why?** _____
   _____
   _____
   _____
   _____
   _____

Remember, Jesus will never invite you to go somewhere that He has not already gone. He is already there, waiting for you. Follow His lead, for there you will see His nature and His heart, poured out for those He loves. Poured out for you.

> "If anyone loves me, he will obey my teaching. My Father will love him, and we will come to him and make our home with him."
> John 14:23

Day Five

The Cloud of Glory

Yesterday we learned that during the most sacred Old Testament

atonement ritual, no one except the High Priest

could enter the sanctuary—this was a job for him

alone. And yet, even though this set-apart man

entered the very Holy of Holies, he still was not

permitted to see the Almighty face-to-face.

> "Who can stand in the presence of the Lord, this holy God?"
>
> I Samuel 6:20

1. **Read Leviticus 16:12-13. What obscured the High Priest's view inside the Holy of Holies on the Day of Atonement?** _____

   _____

2. **Read Leviticus 16:2. What did the incense obscure?** _____

   _____

3. **What would be the consequence if the High Priest entered without this cover? Why do you think this would be true?**

   _____
   _____
   _____
   _____

4. **Read Judges 13:17-24 and Luke 2:9. Who did these people see and what were their reactions?** _____

   _____
   _____
   _____
   _____

Entering the presence of the Most High is deadly. Just one

moment in His radiant glory would physically overwhelm us. The sight

of Him would so strike us to the core at the revelation of our own

"No one can
see my face
and live."
Exodus 33:30

wretchedness, that we physically could not bear it.

Even coming into contact with God's personal

messengers was too close for comfort for the Judean

shepherds. In the words of Oswald Chambers, "when [someone] sees

himself in the light of the Lord, the shame and the horror and the

desperate conviction come home."[53]

5. Read Exodus 24:9-11. Record your thoughts. _____

_____

_____

At the confirmation of His covenant with Israel, God welcomed

the new leadership of Israel into His Presence on Mount Sinai. These

men beheld, *chazah*, the Lord. Yet they didn't actually see His tangible,

physical features with their eyes. You see, *chazah* means to behold,

perceive or receive visions;[54] it is often used in

the testimony of God's prophets such as

Isaiah (1:1) and Amos (1:1). Instead, these

men were blessed to experience God's

The words of
Amos...which he
envisioned (*chazah*)
in visions...
Amos 1:1 NAS

Presence and gaze at the ground upon which He stood. That in itself was more than enough to have brought them to death. But it still wasn't close enough for Moses, not after all he had been through with his Lord.

6. **Read Exodus 3:2-6, 24:15-18, 32:11-14, 33:7-11, and 34:33-35. Describe the nature of Moses' tangible fellowship with the Lord.** _____

_____
_____

7. **✳ Read Exodus 33:15-23. Share your thoughts:** _____

_____
_____

Moses was incomprehensibly intimate with God. He spent weeks on the mountaintop in God's Presence, actually glowing from his proximity to the Almighty. Moses conversed with God the way we do with a dear friend; he reasoned with Him as we would a business partner. Yet Moses still hadn't literally *seen* His Lord. He hadn't watched God's lips form His promises, or His eyes flash with fury. And when God finally obliged Moses' plea to be seen, He knew this passionately devoted man could bear only to view His back.

8. **Read Job 42:1-5 and Hebrews 11:24-28. Based on what you know about Job and Moses, how do you think they were able to "see" the invisible God?** _____

_____
_____

None of us have seen God's face, but we have seen His Glory—

in the creation all around us and in the way

> "When he looks at Me, he sees the One who sent Me."
> John 12:45

He works in our lives. But that just didn't

seem to be enough for us. So God sent His

Son, the perfect representation of Himself, to walk and talk alongside us.

Today, through Scripture, we can observe and grasp the nature of God.

We can marvel that people before us actually touched Christ's hands and

gazed into His eternal eyes. And—if we don't obscure our view with the

details of our days—we, too, can see God in our lives. One day, in the

> For now we see in a mirror dimly, but then face to face.
> I Corinthians 13:12
> NAS

life to come, purified of our wretchedness,

we shall see Him face-to-face. Can you

imagine?

But on *Yom Kippur*, in the confines of the Holy of Holies, the

High Priest could not bear to even catch a glimpse of Almighty. His

vision had to be obscured. Even so, while the smoky incense blinded the

High Priest, it also enveloped him with the picture and fragrance of the

Christ to come—the One whose death and resurrection would not only

draw everyone inside the veil, but to the very real Face of God.

Week Six

The Sacrifice

> "For the life of a creature is in the blood, and I have given it to you to make atonement for yourselves on the altar; it is the blood that makes atonement for one's life."
>
> Leviticus 17:11

The blood sacrifice is perhaps the easiest aspect of the *Yom Kippur* ritual to which Christians can relate. After all, the fact that Jesus died for the sins of all humanity is fundamental to the faith. The Son of God died on the Cross, shedding His blood for our atonement, tasting the death we each deserve. And yet, considering the Cross is perhaps the most overwhelmingly difficult thing a person can do. This is why many true believers *accept* the Cross but cannot bring themselves to *explore* it. It is why many people experienced such vivid pain in viewing Mel Gibson's *The Passion of the Christ.* We came face to face with the brutality endured by Jesus on each of our behalf.

But if we choose to accept, yet never explore, the details of Christ's sacrificial act, we miss out on so very much. We miss discovering for ourselves Jesus' perfect fulfillment of the Law given all the way back in the Sinai. We miss the details that make what He did for you and me so perfectly powerful and precious. And we miss the deepened relationship we can experience with the Creator and Savior of the world as a result of these personal revelations.

Finally, central to this particular study, exploring the Cross in terms of *Yom Kippur* reveals to us how Christ binds together biblical Judaism and the Gospel of Christianity into one complete faith.

Day One

Shedding the Blood

We begin this week with the slaughter of the sacrifice. It is a rather abrupt way to start, I know. There's no build up, no emotional preparation. But so it was with the disciples. No matter how many times Jesus explained that He would be handed over to death, they didn't get it. In less than twenty-four hours, they swung from disputing which of them would become Jesus' right-hand man, to shell-shocked disbelief at watching Him endure a gruesome death.

> "This annual atonement must be made with the blood of the atoning sin offering for the generations to come. It is most holy to the Lord."
> Exodus 30:10

So it was on the Day of Atonement. The gentle lamb, designated by lot as the one "For the Lord," was led away, a lamb to the slaughter. And so we watch Jesus, the final, divinely perfect atonement Sacrifice, in light of the *Yom Kippur* ritual, step by painful step. As you write the following verses, picture the scene in your mind...

FIRST, the High Priest led the perfect lamb to the altar.

1. **Complete Isaiah 53:7:** *...He was led*_____

_____

_____

2. **Complete Matthew 27:31:** *...Then*_____

_____

_____

SECOND, the priests tied the lamb to a ring on the altar's north side.

3. **Complete Mark 15:22:** *They*_____

_____

_____

> *Skull ("calvary" in Latin and "golgotha" in Hebrew) Hill still exists, and is situated on what would have been the North side of the Temple, near the Damascus gate.*[55]

THIRD, the priests bound the lamb by his front and hind legs, securing it to the place of execution.

4. **Complete Acts 2:23:** *...you, with the help of*_____

_____

_____

FOURTH, according to Kosher rules for slaughter, the lamb was fully conscious when it was killed.

5. **Complete Matthew 27:34:** *There*_____

_____

_____

FIFTH, the High Priest collected the blood for the atonement ritual in a golden vessel; the rest he poured at the foot of the altar.

6. **Complete Luke 22:44:** *And*_____

_____

_____

7. **Complete Mark 14:24:** *"This*_____

_____

_____

On the morning of *Yom Kippur*, the priests led

the sacrificial lamb to the North side of the altar.

> Then they led Him away to crucify Him.
> Matthew 27:31b

> Carrying His own cross, He went out to the place of the Skull.
> John 19:17

Jesus allowed His accusers to

lead Him to the North side of the Temple, where He knew

He would become the ultimate blood sacrifice.

The High Priest bound the front and hind

legs of the sacrificial lamb.

> They killed him by hanging him on a tree.
> Acts 10:39

The Roman officials nailed Jesus' hands and

feet to the Cross.

According to Old Testament kosher rules

for food and sacrifice, the sacrificial animal had

to be fully conscious when it was slain.

> Then they
> offered Him
> wine mixed with
> myrrh, but He
> did not take it.
> Mark 15:23

Jesus refused to consume anything that would dull

the full force of His crucifixion—He endured undiminished agony for you.

The leftover sacrificial blood was poured out

at the base of the altar.

> "This is my blood of
> the covenant, which
> is poured out for
> many for the
> forgiveness of sins."
> Matthew 26:28

Jesus' blood was poured out for you and for me

on His altar at Calvary, and the flow continues to purify

anyone who chooses to be washed in it.

Everything about Jesus' death fit the requirements of the Law.

8. **Write out 1 Peter 1:18-19, substituting "you," "you were," and "your" with "I," "I was," and "my."** _____

_____

_____

_____

_____

_____

"Look! The Lamb of God, who takes away the sin of the world!" John 1:29

Day Two

Sprinkling

Has it ever struck you as odd, as you read the words of Peter or the author of Hebrews, that believers are *sprinkled* with the blood of Christ? This wording is no mere poetry. These Jewish men understood that Jesus was our sin offering, and they knew that the blood of sin offerings was not brushed or poured, but sprinkled on the altar.

> He shall dip his finger into the blood and sprinkle it before the Lord...
>
> Leviticus 4:17

1. **Read Hebrews 11:28. When was the first time the Israelites were to sprinkle blood to save themselves from death?** _____
    _____
    _____

2. **Read Exodus 24:1-8 and Hebrews 9:19. Describe the next time blood was sprinkled on their behalf.** _____
    _____
    _____
    _____
    _____

On the eve of the last, deadly plague, the Israelites sprinkled the blood of lambs on their doorposts, shielding them from the Angel of Death. Soon after, in the freedom of the desert, Moses sprinkled God's written Word and His people with blood, confirming the nation's covenant with the Almighty. This blood was sprinkled using hyssop,

water and scarlet wool, pointing to the coming Messiah and His new

> ...to Jesus, the mediator of a new covenant, and to the sprinkled blood that speaks a better word than the blood of Abel.
>
> Hebrews 12:24

covenant: the *branch* from the root of Jesse

would become living *water*, covering our *scarlet*

sins with His own *blood*.

3. **Read Leviticus 4:18 and 16:15. What is a striking difference between the blood of ordinary sin offerings and of the sin offering on *Yom Kippur*?** _____

_____

_____

4. **Read Hebrews 9:12. How did Jesus' sacrifice satisfy the law of atonement forever?** _____

_____

_____

_____

5. **Read Leviticus 16:14-15. How many times did the High Priest sprinkle the blood of the people's sin offering on the Ark of the Covenant (after the initial sprinkling in front of it)?** _____

_____

Seven times the High Priest sprinkled the lamb's blood on the

seat of God's mercy—not outside on the sacrificial altar, but in the very

Holy of Holies. There is a tremendous amount of symbolism ascribed to

the number seven. Because of the important situations in which God

used the number—Creation, certain sacrifices, cleansing regulations, and more—seven symbolizes everything from completion to punishment, penitence to purification, perfection to renewal. But seven's most incredible significance—especially on the Day of Atonement—is its very *definition*.

6. **Read Genesis 21:31. What did Abraham call the place where he and Abimelech made their covenant?** _____

Beersheba, a city at the southern edge of Israel, literally means "well" or "pit" (*beer*) "of the sevenfold oath" (*sheba*). This translation may seem a bit odd, since *sheba* is simply the word for "seven," not "oath." But *sheba* is derived from the root *shaba*, which means to complete, to swear, or to bind with an oath. *Shaba* "was the giving of one's unbreakable word that he would faithfully perform a promised deed or that he would not harm his partner."[56]

> The Lord will establish you as a holy people to Himself, as He swore (*shaba*) to you, if you keep the commandments of the Lord your God and walk in His ways.
>
> Deuteronomy 28:9 NAS

Seven, referred to as the "perfect number," is most perfect when it refers to the perfect promise of God Himself. And that is precisely what we see with the *Yom Kippur* lamb. With that seventh swift rotation of the High Priest's wrist and thumb, the blood he sprinkled from his forefinger[57] completely purified the penitent children of Israel, taking on the punishment they deserved. The seven sprinklings marked God's oath to His people to forgive their sin for yet another year.

The image of those perfect drops of blood sprinkling on the mercy seat brings to mind other drops of perfect blood, those that dripped from the broken body of the Messiah as He shed His blood for us. But instead of counting the seven sprinklings out loud as the High Priest did, Jesus uttered seven different phrases during His atonement sacrifice.

7. **Read the following verses, given in chronological order. Picture the physical condition of your Savior as He uttered these words about your sin and His love. Luke 23:34, Luke 23:43, John 19:26-27, Matthew 27:46, John 19:28, John 19:30, and Luke 23:46.**

As the High Priest counted off each sprinkle of perfect blood, he prayed that the lamb's blood would be enough, that it would satisfy the debt. As Jesus uttered His seven phrases from the Cross, He knew His blood was enough. God's oath, His Perfect Promise, had been kept. The penalty of sin had been paid. It truly was finished, forever.

8. **Read 1 Peter 1:1-2 aloud.** Grace and peace be yours in *abundance*.

Day Three

Cleansing the Temple

After atoning for the sins of the people, the High Priest cleansed

the Tent of Meeting and the Holy Place with the same perfect blood.

You see, it wasn't enough to

simply purify the people; the

place that housed their worship

required decontamination as

well.

> "...He is to do the same for the
> Tent of Meeting, which is among
> them in the midst of their
> uncleanness. Then he shall come
> out to the altar that is before the
> Lord and make atonement for it..."
>
> Leviticus 16:16,18

1. **Read Matthew 21:12-13 and John 2:13-17. How and why did Jesus cleanse the Temple prior to His atonement for the people?** _____

    _____

    _____

    _____

2. **Read Matthew 26:61 and John 2:19-21. Describe Jesus' ultimate cleansing of the Temple.** _____

    _____

    _____

The moneychangers and pigeon sellers were gouging those who

had come to worship, and their striving for personal gain contaminated

the very essence of the Temple and its holy Occupant. But Jesus'

cleansing of the Temple area was just foreshadowing. His ultimate cleansing of the Temple was its destruction. Jesus' death marked the end

of the division between God and man. And so, after the Romans

> I did not see a
> temple in the city,
> because the Lord
> Almighty and the
> Lamb are its
> temple.
>
> Revelation 21:22

destroyed the Temple forty years later, God prohibited the rebuilding of the obsolete structure. Jesus had become the Temple; no stones could contain Him—neither those of the

Temple, nor those of the grave.

3. **Read Ephesians 2:21-22 and 1 Peter 2:5. What is another entity that replaced the physical structure of the Temple?** _____

_____

4. **Why do you think this "structure" requires cleansing?** _____

_____

_____

5. **Of what things must it be cleansed?** _____

_____

_____

_____

The Lord no longer dwells within earthly tapestries and gold, nor

does He reside within the confines of bricks and mortar. The church—

the people, not the buildings—has

replaced the physical Temple. As we

worship and serve together, the Spirit of

> "For where two or
> three come together in
> my name, there am I
> with them."
>
> Matthew 18:20

the Living God dwells among us. What an amazing truth; one that we should never, ever, take for granted.

Unfortunately, if this new temple *were* a physical structure, it would have collapsed long ago. The envy, pride and factions that plague the church today has left us structurally unsound and in dire need of purification and reconciliation. The eternal Lamb prayed for our unity (John 17:20-21), and then cleansed us with His blood. Whether it is within your family, a small group, your home church, or the body of believers as a whole, please allow Christ to cleanse your temple, starting with you.

> Make every effort to live in peace with all men and be holy; without holiness no one will see the Lord.
>
> Hebrews 12:14

6. **Read 1 Corinthians 6:19. There is an even more intimate temple replacement than the living church. What is your personal place of worship as the result of Christ's sacrifice?** _____
   _____

7. **Read Galatians 2:20 and John 14:16-20. What does this personal temple mean for the life of a believer?** _____
   _____
   _____

The church body is not the only temple built for worshiping the

> For we are the temple of the living God.
>
> 2 Corinthians 6:16

Lord. Nor is Jesus the only individual whose

body replaced the Jerusalem Temple. Each believer is a personal house of worship. God Himself dwells *within* you! It is too awesome a gift, too marvelous to comprehend, yet it is true.

Unfortunately, the way we live our lives reveals how unable—or unwilling—we are to accept this truth. Think of all the things we allow to corrupt our bodies—lust, gluttony, neglect of our health, absorbing sinful things with our eyes and ears. Yet we are often puzzled when we don't feel God's strong Presence within us. If you are feeling that God is distant, ask yourself if your temple is a place where you would expect Jesus to take up residence.

> Since we have these promises, dear friends, let us purify ourselves from everything that contaminates body and spirit, perfecting holiness out of reverence for God.
>
> 2 Corinthians 7:1

The crazy thing is that He wants to be there, no matter what the pollution is. The even crazier thing is that He has already paid for the cleaning service—with His own blood. We just need to give the Purifier access to the filth.

8. ✳ **Is your temple in need of cleansing today? From what do you need to be cleansed? Will you accept Jesus' perfect, loving cleansing of your life?** _____

_____

Day Four

The Death of the High Priest

There is a popular "urban legend" floating around about the Old

Testament High Priest. People say that when he entered the Holy of

Holies to make atonement on *Yom Kippur*, he did so with a rope tied

around his ankle. That way, the other priests could pull him out if God

struck him dead. It's quite a dramatic image, but unfortunately there is no biblical reference or historical evidence to support it. Scholars explain that it simply wasn't feasible—the veil

> "You must not defile the Israelites' holy offerings, so that you will not die."
> Numbers 18:32
> HCSB

was too thick and labyrinthine to drag someone out like that.

But what if the High Priest *had* died inside the Holy of Holies?

What would have happened? Would his body remain until the next year?

Would his oldest son be immediately anointed so he could complete the

ritual and drag his father out? But then the son would be defiled by his

father's corpse even before he started. The scenario is a legal minefield!

Well, on Calvary, our Great High Priest *did* die while making His

atoning sacrifice on our behalf. Jesus' death as our High Priest actually

points to His redemptive work just as much as His death as our Sacrifice.

1. **Read Numbers 35:22-32 and Joshua 20:1-6. What is the significance of the death of the High Priest?**

    _____

    _____

    _____

    _____

2. **How does this relate to you in relation to Jesus Christ?** ____

    _____

    _____

    _____

    _____

God's Law provided that those guilty of manslaughter may flee to

a city of refuge. They were allowed to live there free from vengeance on

the part of the victim's family. Then, upon the death of the high priest

serving at the time of the murder, the guilty party was to be restored to

his own land in his hometown—free of punishment. Isn't this you and

me?

Our sinful nature as human beings separated us from God.

Mercifully, the Lord allowed us to live, but it is a life of exile – life outside His Presence. And, just like those in the cities of refuge, we are

not simply guilty of "incidental" sins. We are each guilty of *murder*.

3. Whose life is each one of us guilty of taking? _____

4. What family member would be justified in taking revenge on us for our guilt? _____

_____

Incredibly, the very Father who cries out for vengeance has

Himself spared us from the death penalty. Even more incredible is that,

since the One we put to death was also the Great High Priest, we are

allowed to return home without delay. The

Son's death – which we ourselves caused –

actually frees us from a life of spiritual exile

instead of condemning us to it.

> "May you be richly rewarded by the Lord, the God of Israel, under whose wings you have come to take refuge."
>
> Ruth 2:12

5. Read Luke 15:11-32. What parallels do you see here to the return from the city of refuge? _____

_____

_____

6. Read Isaiah 62:4-5, Hosea 14:4 and Zephaniah 3:17. Upon our return home to the Lord after our waywardness, both here and in Luke 15, what is the nature of God's response to us? _____

_____

_____

We are the ultimate prodigals. Not only have we gone our own

way, but we are guilty of the murder of God's only Son. Amazingly,

> "'But we had to celebrate and be glad, because this brother of yours was dead and is alive again; he was lost and is found.'"
>
> Luke 15:32

following Calvary and the death of

Jesus the Great High Priest, we were

permitted to return home to our

Father. And not amid hushed

whispers about our sordid past. No, despite our bloodguilt, we are

actually welcomed to the banquet table of the very One we have

wronged. Not grudgingly, but with great love and delight, singing and

rejoicing.

Are you still living in a city of refuge, exiled from God? If so, it is

by your own choosing. Have you returned home, yet still shield your

face for fear of accusation? You are the only one pointing fingers

anymore.

Stop. Leave your

isolation and loneliness and

come to the banquet table.

Bask in the deep love and

delight of your Host.

> "I will surely gather them from all the lands where I banish them in my furious anger and great wrath; I will bring them back to this place and let them live in safety. I will rejoice in doing them good and will assuredly plant them in this land with all my heart and soul."
>
> Jeremiah 32:37,41

Day Five

The Scapegoat

The only time in all of Scripture that *kippur* refers to atonement

through anything other than blood is in Leviticus 16:10. On *Yom Kippur*,

even the shedding of perfect blood in God's very Presence wasn't

enough. To complete their expiation, God

required that the people physically place

their sins upon the second perfect lamb

and banish it into the wilderness. This

exceptional usage of *kippur* is explained by

> "The goat chosen by lot as the scapegoat shall be presented alive before the Lord to be used for making atonement."
>
> Leviticus 16:10

the Jewish scholar Ibn Ezra this way: "...the goat itself takes on itself the

expiation."[58] Isn't that exactly what Jesus did on Calvary?

1. **Read Leviticus 16:21. On what part of the scapegoat was the High Priest to place the sins of the people?** _____

   _____

2. **Read Matthew 21:42 and Luke 20:17. Quoting Zechariah 4:7 and Psalm 118:22, what does Jesus call Himself?**

   _____

3. **Look at Week One, Day Two. What is the meaning of *avon*, the word for "sins" used in Leviticus 16:21?** _____

   _____

The Hebrew word for head, *rosh*, is the very same word used for capstone or cornerstone, used by the Old Testament prophets to predict the Messiah's position as the head of God's kingdom. During His Passion week, Jesus made it clear that He was this cornerstone, this

> "The stone which the builders rejected, the same is become the head of the corner."
>
> Matthew 21:42 KJV

Head. Indeed, it was upon His own Head that the sum of all our sins, and all the punishment they deserve, was placed.

4. **Look up Daniel 9:4-5, which was part of the actual confession on *Yom Kippur*.[59] Now imagine placing your hands on the head of Jesus, and say aloud Daniel's confession, replacing "we" with "I."**

5. **Read Leviticus 16:10. In order to make expiation for the people, where was the scapegoat to take their sin? _____**

6. **In Leviticus 16:8,10 and 26, does your Bible give another name for the scapegoat, or provide a note about the word's derivation? What is it? _____**

7. **Read Isaiah 53:12, 1 Peter 2:24, and Matthew 27:45-46. When did Jesus become the scapegoat of the world? _____**
   _____
   _____

8. **Why did the Father turn away from Jesus during those three hours? _____**
   _____
   _____
   _____

The Hebrew word translated in most Bibles as "scapegoat" or the "goat of removal" is *azazel*, the exact meaning of which is uncertain. Some say *azazel* refers to the inaccessible wilderness to which the scapegoat took the people's sins. Or, since *ez* means "goat" and *azal* means "to go away,"

> "The goat will carry on itself all their sins to a solitary place.
> Leviticus 16:22

others explain that *azazel* simply described the goat and its task. Finally, some scholars report that *azazel* is the name various cultures gave to the ancient demonic ruler of the wilderness.[60] In truth, all of these meanings fit, considering that the scapegoat took away the people's sins into the wilderness, depositing them on Satan's doorstep.[k]

As Jesus hung on His Cross, He bore the sins of the entire human race upon Himself. The sky turned black, for the Father had turned away from His only, beloved Son. He simply couldn't bear to look at such filth. Our filth. Jesus was willing to be covered in our

> ...the Lord has laid on Him the iniquity of us all.
> Isaiah 53:6

wretchedness, so that we might be covered with His righteousness. And so, for those last three hours of His mortal life, Jesus was separated from His daddy, the Most Holy, Almighty God. Can you imagine a

---

[k] In modern Hebrew, the phrase *"lekh la-azazel"* is actually translated as "get lost" or "go to hell" (Fox, E., 1995). Isn't that exactly where Jesus took our sins, depositing them there forever?

more solitary place?

9. **Read Leviticus 16:26. Describe the situation for the man who released the scapegoat into the wilderness.** _____

_____

_____

10. **How does this parallel the standing of a person who has been walking with sin, apart from God?** _____

_____

_____

_____

Just like the man who accompanied the scapegoat into the wilderness, we must release our walk with sin. We must turn back and bathe in the Savior's blood in order to join the rest of the redeemed. And then we are to be washed through baptism, publicly announcing our acceptance of Him as our substitute.

> "'And now what are you waiting for? Get up, be baptized and wash your sin away, calling on His name.'"
>
> Acts 22:16

There is no way around it. Your sin led Jesus to a painfully solitary place, yet He shouldered your burden willingly, lovingly.

11. ✳ **Is there a sin of which you cannot let go? Picture yourself handing it over to the eternal Scapegoat, and allow Him to carry it away...**

Week Seven

The Resurrection

> For if, while we were enemies we were reconciled to God
> through the death of His Son, then how much more,
> having been reconciled, will we be saved by His life!
> Romans 5:10 HCSB

How perfectly and beautifully did Jesus fulfill His Father's Law of
Atonement! We have witnessed through Scripture both how Jesus was
perfectly foreshadowed and how He perfectly fulfilled every key aspect
of the Jewish Day of Atonement ritual—the Tabernacle in which it took
place, the High Priest who conducted it, and the Blood that sealed it.

But as perfect and final as it was, Christ's death was not the
completion of His atoning sacrifice. Why is the resurrection so vital, so
necessary to Christ's redemptive work? At a most fundament level,
Jesus' resurrection assures our eternal life. First, His death purchased our
earthly pardon from sin. Jesus' sacrifice allows us to live on earth in
communion with God. But His resurrection went beyond the atonement
requirement. When Jesus conquered His own death, He conquered our

as well, allowing us to live beyond the grave for an eternity of communion with the Triune Lord.

Just as importantly, Jesus' resurrection confirmed His identity. As many Jewish scholars rightly argue, the followers of all false messiahs abandon their leader upon his death. Death exposed their illegitimacy, their inability to fulfill their claims. Yet this argument, often used to deny Christ, actually proves His identity.

Upon Jesus' death, all of His followers had fled. Even Peter, the "rock," insisted he never even knew Jesus—three times in a row. And yet, on the third day after the crucifixion, something happened that brought them all back. Something so dramatic, so convincing, that not only did all of Jesus' followers regroup, but thousands more immediately came to faith in Him as the Messiah. What could it have been? What could have been so convincing *after* Jesus' "failure" that those who had never seen Him before would bend their knee, and those who had run away would come back and lay down their lives for Him?

Simple. They had seen with their own eyes that this crucified dead man was again alive. He was the real thing. The true Anointed One. He was—and is—the risen Messiah. And, as you will see, the

Messiah's resurrection has everything to do with the Day of Atonement. It is foreshadowed in parts of the ritual, and it perfected and eternalized Jesus' mission as both our Great High Priest and our perfect blood Sacrifice.

Day One

The Rising

The sacrificial lambs on the Day of Atonement did not literally

rise from the dead. Yet there are striking aspects of Christ's resurrection

that point directly back to *Yom Kippur*. And

these aspects of the Old Testament atonement

ritual have everything to do with the eternal

nature of Jesus' mission.

> After the suffering of His soul, He will see the light of life and be satisfied.
>
> Isaiah 53:11a

1. **Read Leviticus 16:23. After conducting the blood sacrifice and banishing the scapegoat to the wilderness, what did the High Priest do to symbolize the atonement process was complete?**

   _____

   _____

2. **Read John 20:3-9. Describe what John and Peter found when they looked into Jesus' tomb.** _____

   _____

   _____

   _____

Upon completing the atonement sacrifice in the very Holy of

> "...you will not abandon me to the grave, nor will you let your Holy One see decay."
>
> Psalm 16:10

Holies, the High Priest shed his linen

garments, leaving them behind for good. As

we have studied, the Great High Priest

conducted the ultimate atonement ritual not simply in God's Presence but as God Himself. And when He was done with the death it required, the Christ shed those strips of linen, folding them neatly and leaving His grave clothes behind forever.

3. **Read John 20:10-12. What did Mary Magdalene see that first Easter Sunday?** _____

_____

Sketch what she saw in the left-hand square below.

#3	#5

4. **Does this visual remind you of something else we have studied? If so, what?** _____

5. **Read Exodus 25:17-20. Sketch the atonement cover in the right-hand square above.**

When the grieving Mary Magdalene peered into Jesus' tomb, she was greeted by two angels, sitting at either end of Jesus' neatly folded burial garments. After all her time learning at the Rabbi's feet, this encounter in the tomb must have triggered a vivid mental image. At each

end of the glorious mercy seat sat a cherub, with wings spread to shield

the earthly throne of God. And it was on

Yom Kippur that the blood of a perfect lamb

was sprinkled on this golden atonement

cover.

> "…Why do you look for the living among the dead? He is not here; he has risen!"
> Luke 24:5-6

On that first Easter morning, living angels sat at either end of

Jesus empty grave clothes, proclaiming what we now know to be true.

Jesus Himself had become the living Mercy Seat, the point at which we

receive the remission of sins in the very Presence of God Almighty at

every moment for all time.

6. **Review Week Two, Day One. What were key functions of the mercy seat?** _____

   _____

7. **Read (a) Matthew 28:18, (b) Acts 5:31, (c) Ephesians 3:12, and (d) 1 Peter 1:23. What does Jesus' resurrection as the mercy seat mean for us?**

   a. _____

   b. _____

   c. _____

   d. _____

With Jesus as the living, resurrected Mercy Seat, everything about

God's covenant is now alive. The source of authority for judgment and forgiveness is now our living, breathing Savior, whose blood purchased

> "I am the Living One; I was dead, and behold I am alive forever and ever! And I hold the keys of death and Hades."
> Revelation 1:18

our pardon, and whose resurrection makes that pardon an ongoing—not annual— reality for those who would approach Him.

Second, God's Word is no longer just the written account of His covenant with His people, nor is it concealed any longer by the gilded lid. The Testimony is the living, breathing Son who not only walked the earth, but now strides across the Heavens!

> For the word of God is living and active...
> Hebrews 4:12

Finally, while God used to address the Israelites from that secluded seat of mercy, He now communes intimately with every man,

> "...I am in my Father, and you are in Me, and I am in you."
> John 14:20

woman and child through His living Son.

The Risen Son is the resurrected Mercy Seat. He is the living, breathing dispenser of mercy, truth and fellowship with God. And He is always straining forward, waiting to lavish these gifts upon all who would approach Him.

Day Two

The Ascension

The physical point of forgiveness on the Day of Atonement—the

mercy seat—was not the only aspect of *Yom Kippur* that brings special

meaning to the Messiah's victory over

the grave. Part of the atonement ritual

itself also foretold His ascension into

the heavens.

"The priest is to turn all of it
into smoke upon the
slaughter site, for an offering-
up, a fire-offering of soothing
favor for YHWH."
Leviticus 1:9
The Schocken Bible

1. **Read Leviticus 16:24. What ritual did the High Priest conduct
    after redressing in his regal garments?** _____
    _____

2. **Review Week One, Day Four. What was symbolism of the
    burnt offering?** _____
    _____

3. **Read Mark 16:19. Consider the burnt offering and how it relates
    to Jesus.** _____
    _____
    _____

Olah, the Hebrew word translated as burnt offering, literally

means "that which goes up," because the smoke rises to the Lord.

During the *olah*, the sacrifice was burned completely, symbolizing

complete surrender and dedication to God.[61]   On the Day of

Atonement, the High Priest sent up this pleasing aroma to God after

offering the perfect sacrifice and shedding his clothes of humility. But

after offering Himself and shedding His grave clothes, Jesus didn't simply

present a *symbol* that rose to the heavens. He Himself became "that

which goes up" by conquering death and returning to His Father's side.

4. **Read Leviticus 16:24. What did God say was the purpose of the burnt offering on *Yom Kippur*?** _____
    _____

5. **What do you think this might mean, since the sin offering had already been offered in the Holy of Holies?** _____
    _____
    _____

According to biblical scholars, the burnt offering did not actually

atone for sin, as the English translation implies. Rather, it provided the

Israelites with *assurance* that their sin was covered (*kaphar*) in the eyes of

the Almighty because of the atoning blood.

On Easter, Jesus' resurrection and ascension assure us that His

perfect sacrifice for your atonement and mine was accepted. If it were

not so, Jesus would still be in that grave,

"I am returning to my
Father and your
Father, to my God
and your God."

John 20:17

decayed by death. But His complete surrender

for us was received as a pleasing aroma to the

Father, and He literally became "that which goes up," conquering death

and rising to the right hand of the Almighty!

One day, we too will rise from death to dwell with the Father and

Son in the heavens. In the meantime, how can we live our lives as burnt

offerings to our Lord?

6. **Read Deuteronomy 6:5 and Jeremiah 29:13. In what way should
    our surrender to God mirror the burnt offering?** _____
    _____
    _____
    _____

7. **Read Isaiah 48:10 and Malachi 3:2-4. How is the mode of the
    burnt offering—burning—reflected in our walks with the Lord?**
    _____
    _____
    _____

The burnt offering is often referred to as the sacrifice of

completion, pointing both to the state of the offeror's submission to

God, and to the mode of the sacrifice—complete burning. Similarly, the

Lord expects our *complete* surrender to His love for us and to His purpose

for our lives. As we wholly submit to Him, we will certainly experience

> ...offer your
> bodies as living
> sacrifices, holy and
> pleasing to God...
> Romans 12:1

times of refinement. Times that may not be

pleasant—indeed, that are often quite painful. But

through these times God brings us closer to Himself, and closer to the

person He created us to be. In allowing Him to refine us, our lives will

rise to Him as a pleasing aroma.

> For you, O God, tested us; you refined us like silver...we went through fire and water, but you brought us to a place of abundance.
> Psalm 66:10,12

It must be said, however, that offering

our lives to God for His purposes is *not* what

gains our acceptance before His Throne.

Salvation can be found in nothing other than

our personal acceptance of Christ's blood in exchange for our own.

Instead, our complete consecration to God is a gift of thanksgiving to

Him. And because the Father accepted Jesus' Sacrifice, we now have

access to His Throne, where we may lay our love gift before Him.

8. **Read Hebrews 13:15-16. How can your life rise to God as a pleasing aroma today?** _____

_____

_____

_____

_____

_____

Day Three

The Resurrected High Priest

We have seen that Jesus was our Great High Priest. He offered

the ultimate atonement sacrifice on our behalf—not just in the Presence

of God, but as God Himself made flesh. Further,

unlike the earthly high priests, Jesus' ministry did

not end with His death. Instead, because of the

Resurrection, our Great High Priest was made

even greater *after* He died.

> ...we have a great high priest who has gone through the heavens...
>
> Hebrews 4:14

1. **Read Psalm 110:4. How long will Jesus serve as humanity's High Priest?** _____

2. **Read Hebrews 10:12. Where does Jesus perform His priestly ministry?** _____
   _____

King David proclaimed that the Messiah would be a priest in the

order of Melchizedek, and the Resurrection made it so. The Great High

Priest is eternal—and thus an earthly mediator between God and man is

no longer needed. The Divine Mediator confers directly with the One

who holds the universe in His Hands. And He yearns to share your

heart's cry.

3. **Read Hebrews 2:17, Hebrews 7:25, and Hebrews 8:6. In what ways does the resurrected Jesus serve us as High Priest?** ___

_____

_____

_____

4. **Read Exodus 28:29-30. Reflect on the significance of these verses when considering that Jesus serves as your** _eternal_ **Great High Priest.** _____

_____

_____

_____

You will recall that the primary duties of the earthly High Priest were to offer sacrifices on behalf of the people, to intercede for them before God, and to reveal to them God's wisdom. By performing these functions, the High Priest mediated the covenant between God and man.

Now, as part of the New Covenant, the resurrected High Priest eternally redeems you and never ceases interceding for you. Every moment that Jesus speaks with the Father about the "grand plan," He is

> ...because Jesus lives forever, He has a permanent priesthood.
> Hebrews 7:24

holding your name over His heart. _Your name._ The resurrected Messiah, the One to whom every knee in creation will bow, holds you over His heart when He makes every single decision. Next time you're feeling insignificant, remember _that._

5. **Read Numbers 3:10 and read Hebrews 9:7 and 4:16. What is the one thing Jesus provides for us that the earthly High Priest could not?** _____

_____

The mortal High Priest could not provide people access to God, because not even he was allowed to come face-to-Face with the Creator. His sinful nature prevented it. No matter how many sacrifices he made, he was still banished from God's personal Presence. And his forgiven congregation was still forbidden to even come close to the sanctuary.

In divine contrast, our living, risen High Priest sits at the Father's side—not once a year under a shield of incense, but Face-to-Face for all eternity. The resurrected High Priest brings ordinary men and women

> "See, I have placed before you an open door that no one can shut."
> Revelation 3:8

into the very Presence of the Creator. We are no longer forbidden from God's holy court or limited in our access. Instead we are beckoned. You see, not only does Jesus hold you over His heart as He confers with the Almighty, but they both invite you to join the discussion anytime. The only one blocking your way is you.

6. **Read Mark 2:5, Mark 10:16, Luke 22:32, and John 17:15. Visualize your risen Jesus, conferring with His Father, speaking similar personal words about you—requests to the Almighty to forgive you, to bless you, to strengthen you, to protect you.**

7. ✷ As you are visualizing this in your mind, know that it is a personal reality in Heaven. How does this make you feel about Jesus and about yourself? _____

_____

_____

Your Jesus sits at the right hand of all Authority, the Master of the Universe, pleading on your behalf. Whether your ministry is parenting a child or planting a church, the Wonderful Counselor is praying for your wisdom. Whether your sin is swearing or stealing, the Savior is petitioning for your forgiveness. Whether your trial is dealing with colic, cancer or company cutbacks, the Deliverer is asking God to strengthen you, knowing your deep ache because He created the heart that feels it.

8. ✷ Read Philippians 4:6-7. What is the burden of your heart today? _____

_____

_____

Present it to your Great High Priest, Jesus the Messiah, and know that He is petitioning the God of all Creation on your behalf at this very moment.

Day Four

The Resurrected Sacrifice

Through His resurrection, Jesus conquered death, both for

Himself and for all who would believe in Him. And with His ascension,

the Great High Priest returned to His rightful place, the right hand of

God, where He continually mediates for

God's children. Yet our resurrected High

Priest is not the only one sitting at the right

hand of the Almighty. Our Blood

atonement—Jesus the Sacrifice—sits on the

> He entered the Most Holy Place once for all with His own blood, having obtained eternal redemption.
>
> Hebrews 9:12

Throne of Heaven as well. The blood that spilled onto the dusty ground

of Calvary has been revived, and now courses through the veins of the

risen Savior. He is the ultimate Living Sacrifice.

1. **Read Hebrews 9:9-12 and 10:10. What do these verses say about the finality of Jesus' self-sacrifice as compared to the annual** *Yom Kippur* **sacrifice?** _____
   _____
   _____

2. **How do you think the resurrection makes this so?** _____
   _____
   _____
   _____
   _____

3. According to these verses, what does Jesus' blood achieve for believers?

   a. Matthew 26:28 _____

   b. Hebrews 9:14 _____

   c. 1 John 1:7 _____

   d. Colossians 1:20 _____

4. Now, consider each of these aspects in light of the fact that the Blood has risen, making them living, continual gifts of God.

   _____
   _____
   _____
   _____
   _____

The sacrifice is eternal because the Sacrifice is alive. The crucifixion is continual—every sin committed before the Messiah's death, every sin we commit this very day, and every sin committed by our descendants centuries from now, drives the nails into Christ's wrists.

Jesus' *death* is *alive*.

But that means that the

> For Christ died for sins once for all, the righteous for the unrighteous, to bring you to God. He was put to death in the body but made alive by the Spirit.
>
> 1 Peter 3:18

triumph of His death also lives. God's forgiveness is a daily gift. He cleanses us continually as we present ourselves to Him, purifying us from the sins we swore yesterday we wouldn't commit yet again today. We can live every day of our lives at peace with God and with one another—if

we allow Christ's death of reconciliation to live within us and among us.

5. **Read Romans 12:1. How are we to live like Jesus, our Resurrected Sacrifice?** _____

   _____

   _____

6. **Read Colossians 2:13, 20 and Galatians 2:20. Why must we live this way?** _____

   _____

   _____

7. **Read 2 Corinthians 5:14-15 and 1 Peter 4:2. As living sacrifices, then, what should be the focus of our daily lives?** _____

   _____

   _____

   _____

8. **Read Romans 8:13. How are we able to live this way?** _____

   _____

   _____

   _____

As living sacrifices, we must acknowledge that we are dead. Dead

to our sin because we have been redeemed, and dead to ourselves,

because it is no longer our life living within us. A dead body has no

power over itself. Instead, the Holy Spirit lives within us, breathing the

very life into our heart, our mind, and our limbs.

If we allow God's Holy Spirit free reign, He will empower us to

live abundantly for God, rather than meagerly for ourselves. But if we choose instead to squelch Him, we will simply be corpses stumbling

through life, grasping at food that

cannot nourish and shelters that cannot

shield. Why would we – I – you –

choose such an existence?

> And if the Spirit of Him who raised Jesus from the dead is living in you, He who raised Christ from the dead will also give life to your mortal bodies through His Spirit, who lives in you.
>
> Romans 8:11

Jesus' death is very much alive,

and we are alive as well. Alive only by the power of God, and therefore

compelled to live only to the glory of God.

9. ✳ How could you live as a sacrifice for the Lord today? ____

_____
_____
_____
_____
_____

Day Five

The Tabernacle as the Path of Christ

This week, we have journeyed with Jesus to His final

destination—His rightful place at the right Hand of God. Today, we will

open our minds and hearts to the breathtaking

way that the physical path of the atonement

ritual pointed to Jesus' exact steps—from His

earthly lineage all the way to the very Throne of

Heaven.

> They serve at a sanctuary that is a copy and shadow of what is in heaven.
>
> Hebrews 8:5

1. **Label the items of the Tabernacle on the diagram on the next page (refer to Weeks Two and Three if needed).**

2. **Write each of the descriptions/titles of Christ revealed by these verses in their symbolic location on the Tabernacle diagram.**

   a. **John 1:1**   e. **John 6:35**

   b. **John 1:14**   f. **John 8:12**

   c. **John 1:29**   g. **Ephesians 5:2**

   d. **John 4:10**

3. **What do you notice about the shape formed by the objects in the Tent of Meeting and Tabernacle?** _____

The Desert Tabernacle

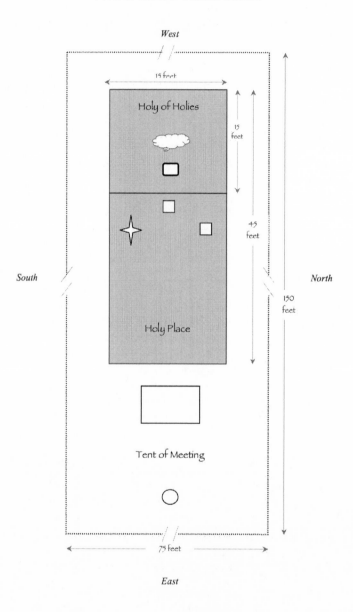

West

15 feet

Holy of Holies

15
feet

45
feet

150
feet

South

North

Holy Place

Tent of Meeting

75 feet

East

4. Read Numbers 2:2-3. Which tribe camped on the eastern (entrance) side of the Tent of Meeting? _____
Write the tribe's name in the appropriate location on the diagram.

5. Read Numbers 3:38. Who camped between the tribe in #4 and the Tent of Meeting entrance? Recall their God-appointed role in the Israelite community. _____
_____
Write their name and role in the appropriate location.

6. Look at your diagram. Approaching the Tabernacle from the East, a person would first encounter the tribe of _____ and then the clan of the _____ on his way to the sacrificial altar.

7. Read Hebrews 7:14. To what tribe did Jesus belong? _____
_____
Write in Jesus' name on the Tabernacle diagram with His tribe.

8. Read Hebrews 5:5-6. On the Tabernacle diagram, write Jesus' role from this verse in the appropriate location.

9. Read John 12:1,12. When Jesus made His Triumphal Entry into Jerusalem, from what city did He travel? _____

10. If your Bible contains historical maps, find Jerusalem at the time of Christ. Traveling from Bethany to Jerusalem, from what direction would Jesus enter the Holy City? _____

You have been putting together a beautiful picture. Not just a picture of the reality for the desert Israelites, but a picture of the personal Promise for their spiritual descendants—you and me. Imagine gazing down at the Tabernacle and its Cross-shaped contents from above—the

Father's and Son's view—for the two thousand years between the

promise of the true Tabernacle and its fulfillment.

11. ✳ **Ponder all that is revealed in this "God's-eye view." What does it say to your heart and mind about Jesus?** _____

_____

_____

_____

_____

_____

As Jesus entered Jerusalem from the East on Palm Sunday, He

knew that His course fulfilled the symbolic path to the Tabernacle—He

had gazed at it from above since its construction. The Lion of Judah was

born to become the Lord's eternal High Priest, the Living Water, the

Bread of Life, and the Light of the World. And, despite a day filled with

hosannas and palm branches, Jesus knew that the gentle mule He rode

carried Him closer and closer to the altar on which He would become the

final atonement offering for His beloved: you. But Jesus also knew that,

on the other side of that sacrificial altar, He—like the incense that

> For Christ did not enter a man-made sanctuary that was only a copy of the true one; He entered Heaven itself, now to appear for us in God's Presence.
>
> Hebrews 9:24

symbolized Him—would ascend to His rightful place, the Most Holy Place, to the right hand of God.

Week Eight

Acceptance

"...at that time your people—everyone whose name is found written in the book—will be delivered."

Daniel 12:1b

It's over. The High Priest has journeyed from the gate of the Tent of Meeting, and has sacrificed the perfect lamb on the sacrificial altar. He has sprinkled its redeeming blood on the Ark in the Most Holy Place. The scapegoat has taken the people's sins upon itself and carried them into the wilderness. And the smoke from the burnt offering, the flesh of the sacrifice, has risen to the Throne of God. The *Yom Kippur* ritual was over. Or was it?

Jesus, too, had completed His Ritual. He became our Great High Priest and sacrificed His very Self, bearing the weight of all humanity's sin upon His shoulders. He redeemed us all with His perfect Blood not just in the Presence of God *but as God Himself made man.* And, just like that *Yom Kippur* burnt offering, Christ's body rose to the very Throne of Heaven. Not figuratively like the smoke of the charred sacrifice, but literally: the resurrected Messiah rose to walk again with those who would walk with Him, and then ascended into the clouds before their very eyes. Jesus' fulfillment of the atonement ritual was over. Or was it?

Leviticus 16 did not end with the instructions for the burnt offering, and Jesus' Ascension is not the end of His story either. The High Priest had done all that he could do. Jesus completed all that He had come to do.

Yet there was still more to be done.

Day One

Rending the Curtain

Imagine you are the High Priest. You have shuffled your way out of the Holy of Holies, head bowed, shaken by the reality of what you have done and where you have done it. You arrange the burnt offering with trembling hands, praying that God has accepted the most holy blood sacrifice on behalf of all Israel.

> May He remember all your sacrifices and accept your burnt offerings.
>
> Psalm 20:3

1. **Read Leviticus 1:3-4 and Amos 5:22. Is offering the sacrifice enough to secure atonement?** _____

2. **What is vital to the effect of the sacrifice?** _____
_____

In order for a sacrifice to hold any value for the offeror, it had to be accepted by God. Otherwise it was an exercise in futility. The *Yom Kippur* sacrifice was no different, which made the High Priest's job all the more serious. If this atonement sacrifice, offered in God's very Presence, was unacceptable—or presented in an unacceptable manner—then the people would also be unacceptable, still covered with sin and estranged from God.

Mercifully, God did communicate his acceptance of the *Yom Kippur*

sacrifice in a supernatural way. Jewish historians tell us that, even going

back to Solomon's Temple, a priest tied a piece of crimson cloth to the

door of the sanctuary[1] at the beginning of the atonement ritual.[62] The

> Though your sins are like scarlet, they shall be as white as snow; though they are red as crimson, they shall be like wool."
>
> Isaiah 1:18

community received confirmation of their

pardon if the cloth turned white at the

conclusion of the ritual.[63] This is likely the

visual Isaiah was conveying to the people in

Isaiah 1:18. Even more astounding? Jewish tradition says that this

miraculous sign ceased 40 years before the destruction of the Temple,[64]

which occurred in 70 A.D. You do the math.

As dramatic and breathtaking as it must have been to witness the

supernatural bleaching of the wool, think of how much more

breathtaking it must have been to serve in the Temple the day Jesus died.

In fact, breathtaking isn't the word. It was literally *earth shattering*.

3. **Read Matthew 27:51-53 and Luke 23:45. What happened in the Temple when Jesus died?** _____

    _____

    _____

---

[1] Some accounts say it was tied to the neck of the blood sacrifice (Edersheim, 1994).

4. **Did this indicate God's acceptance of Jesus' sacrifice?** _____

_____

5. **Recall the function of the veil. How did its destruction communicate God's acceptance of the Messiah's sacrifice?**

_____

_____

_____

6. **Why do you believe Jesus' death was acceptable to God as our redemptive substitute?** _____

_____

_____

_____

7. **Read John 14:20 and Hebrews 10:19-22. What does God's message of the rent veil communicate to people today?** _____

_____

_____

_____

You will recall that the veil separating the Holy of Holies in the Tabernacle was no breezy cotton curtain, but a 15-foot by 15-foot tapestry that by some accounts was three feet thick. As part of his restoration of the Temple, Herod increased the height of the structure to 90 feet.[65] So the dense veil that hung during Jesus' time was 15 feet by 90 feet—an area of 1,350 square feet! By that time, the veil also hung in a type of labyrinth (or potentially two veils hung together),[66] so that the High Priest could pass through the veil without ever exposing The

Presence. This was not a divider that could tear easily from the bottom, let alone from the top...

Close your eyes and try to picture the magnificent, weighty tapestry, towering ten stories above you. Imagine that you were ministering in the Temple when that mighty

> And behold, the veil of the temple was torn in two from top to bottom; and the earth shook and the rocks were split.
> Matthew 27:51
> NASB

curtain tore apart, the earth shaking beneath your feet. The panic and fear must have been palpable. You could taste it. Death was imminent,

> "I have placed before you an open door that no one can shut."
> Revelation 3:8

for God's Presence was loosed. But for those who in that moment knew the Truth, *life* was imminent, for God's Presence was loosed.

God had accepted the ultimate Sacrifice—not of a perfect animal but of the perfect Man. Under the perfect cover of that Blood, our crimson souls are white as snow. Our Holy Father no longer needs to shelter His Face from His children. His jealous love can no longer be contained. His Presence is no longer kept from us, but kept inside us.

"Oh that you would," pleaded Isaiah. "Oh, *that I have*,"

> "Oh, that you would rend the heavens and come down..."
> Isaiah 64:1

answers the One who split time.

Day Two

The Temple Destroyed

For centuries, God's Presence traveled with His people. The

house of the One True God was carried on the shoulders of men

through the wilderness and into the

Promised Land. Wherever they camped,

He camped, and wherever they walked, He

walked. Even during the reign of David,

God's beloved king, the King of Glory

lived as a nomad on the earth.

> "I have not dwelt in a house from the day I brought the Israelites up out of Egypt to this day. I have been moving from place to place with a tent as my dwelling."
>
> 2 Samuel 7:6

1. **Read 2 Samuel 7:12-13, 1 Kings 5:1-5 and Acts 7:47. Who built the Lord's first "permanent" Temple?** _____

2. **Read 2 Kings 25:8-9 and Jeremiah 52:12-23. What happened to the Temple in approximately 587 B.C.?** _____
   _____
   _____

3. **Read 2 Chronicles 36:22-23. What happened 70 years later?**
   _____
   _____
   _____

4. **Read John 2:20. What did Herod the Great do to the Temple?**
   _____
   _____

David's son Solomon was blessed with the charge of building a glorious Temple for the Lord. And, despite the waxing and waning of Israel's faithfulness, Solomon's Temple survived for more than 350 years. Then, in one fell swoop, King Nebuchadnezzar of Babylon had it pillaged and burned to the ground with the rest of Jerusalem in 587 B.C. Seventy years later, King Cyrus of Persia ordered the Temple rebuilt. It was finally completed during the reign of King Darius in 515 B.C. under the leadership of Ezra and Nehemiah.

During the second century before Christ, Syria ruled over Judea, and King Antiochus defiled the Temple in many ways. The most gut-wrenching for the Israelites was his sacrifice of a pig—an unclean animal—in the very Holy of Holies. A victorious grassroots rebellion allowed, the Jews to rededicate the Temple in 166 B.C. This victory and restoration is what Jews commemorate each year at *Hanukkah*. After that time, Judea lived in relative freedom until Roman occupation began in 63 B.C. Then, to gain popularity among his Jewish subjects, the puppet king Herod the Great spent 46 years—and considerable wealth— reconstructing the Temple beyond even Solomon's imagination.

5. **What does this history say to you about the importance of the Temple to God?** _____

_____

_____

6. **Do you know what happened to the Temple in 70 A.D.?** ___

_____

7. **Was it rebuilt?** _____

In the almost 1,100 years after Solomon first began constructing the Temple, God's earthly dwelling was built, destroyed, rebuilt, damaged, repaired, defiled and rededicated over and over until Rome burned it to the ground in 70 A.D. Yet in the almost 2,000 years since then, God has not provided that one stone of that majestic structure be rebuilt. In fact, with the Dome of the Rock mosque now resting squarely on top of the Temple ruins, rebuilding isn't even an option. Why?

8. **Read 2 Chronicles 7:12 and Jeremiah 26:2. What were the two main purposes of the Jerusalem Temple?** _____

_____

9. **Read Matthew 24:1-3. Who predicted the ultimate and permanent destruction of the Jerusalem Temple?** _____

10. **Read John 2:19-21. What Temple was even more precious to God than the Jerusalem Temple?** _____

11. **Read Mark 16:6. What happened to God's more precious Temple after His "destruction?"** _____

_____

12. **Read John 14:6. What does this say about Jesus as the new Temple?** _____

_____

_____

13. **Think about our study's focus: Jesus' fulfillment of the Day of Atonement. In that light, why do you think God rescued the Temple time and again before Christ, but never again after Him?** _____

_____

_____

_____

Before Jesus, the only way for Israel to remain in fellowship with

God was through the perfect blood sacrifice sprinkled within the Holy of

Holies. And so, time and again, God provided for the Temple's

> He who was seated on the throne said "I am making everything new!"
> Revelation 21:5

rebuilding. But after Jesus, after the perfect Son

of God redeemed all mankind with His own

Blood, the Temple became obsolete. The

annual blood sacrifice was useless, because the eternal one was complete.

God therefore allowed the permanent destruction of the

manmade house of worship that bore His

Name. The new eternal Temple is God's

> And in him you too are being built together to become a dwelling in which God lives by his Spirit.
> Ephesians 2:22

perfect atoning Son. Through the doors of His

Blood, and under the power of His Name,

worshippers can now enter into the very heart of the Father in Heaven.

Day Three

The People's Response

We have focused so exclusively on the work of the High Priest,

the perfect blood he carried, and the One to Whom he presented it, that

it would be easy to assume they were the only

"players" in this life and death drama. But such

an assumption would be a grave mistake for a

person desiring to be reconciled with God.

"On the tenth day of this seventh month hold a sacred assembly."
Numbers 29:7

1. **Read Exodus 23:14-17. What are the three holy days for which God required pilgrimage to Jerusalem?** _____
    _____
    _____

2. **Why do you think God didn't require the people to pilgrimage to Jerusalem for the Day of Atonement?** _____
    _____
    _____

3. **Read Leviticus 23:30. What specific thing does the Lord prohibit on the Day of Atonement?** _____

4. **Do you see any parallels between the people's role on *Yom Kippur* and salvation through Christ?** _____
    _____
    _____
    _____

The children of Israel weren't even invited to attend the act that secured their redemption. And any type of work on that day—even good deeds—meant condemnation and death. Exercising anything other than sober faith and worship on the Day of Atonement was an act of rebellion. But the people's absence and their apparent inactivity did not mean that they had no role.

5. **Read Leviticus 16:29-31. What did the Lord require of the people on the Day of Atonement?** _____

_____

_____

6. **Recall Leviticus 23:30. What would be the consequence if a person did not obey this command?** _____

_____

It didn't matter how flawlessly the High Priest offered the sacrifice. The perfect blood sprinkled in God's Presence meant nothing. And the Almighty's acceptance of the sacrifice was of no consequence. Not if the people failed to honor the atonement. And not if they failed to accept the sacrifice for their own personal sin.

7. **Read John 3:17. Who did Jesus die to save?** _____

8. **Read 2 Peter 3:9. Who does Jesus want to save?** _____

9. **Read Acts 2:21 and Romans 10:9. Does Jesus' desire and ability to save every person mean that everyone is, in fact, saved? What determines individual redemption?** _____

_____

The consequences of dismissing the Old Testament Day of

Atonement were separation from the community and death. Likewise,

> These are written that you may believe that Jesus is the Christ, the Son of God, and that by believing you may have life in His name.
> John 20:31

the consequences of dismissing the Cross are a spiritual disconnection from believers and, ultimately, eternal death. Jesus did all He could do to save you, and the Holy Judge accepted His act of redemption on your behalf. But it

won't mean one iota for you if you don't personally believe in and accept

the sacrifice for yourself.

10. **Read Matthew 7:22-23, Romans 5:1, and Ephesians 2:8-9. What do these verses say about our ability to earn our salvation?** _____

_____

11. **How many good works must we perform in order to make it to heaven?** _____

12. **Read John 6:28-29. What is the only work that assures your salvation?** _____

Selfless acts of compassion for people in our community or

around the world cannot bring us into a saving relationship with God or earn us a spot in heaven. Nor can membership—or even leadership—in

a religious community. We could never do

enough or be enough on our own to earn

standing before the pure, perfect, Holy

Judge.

> Without faith it is impossible to please God, because anyone who comes to him must believe that he exists and that he rewards those who earnestly seek him.
>
> Hebrews 11:6

What was true for the Israelites in

the desert is just as true for mankind today. We must each, as

individuals, accept the Truth of the atoning Sacrifice for ourselves, in our

own hearts, or else our eternal isolation is guaranteed. And there is only

one good work you can perform to assure your place in heaven: To

believe in Jesus the Christ, the One God sent to save you.

13. ✳ **Have you truly believed in and accepted Jesus' sacrifice to atone for your personal sin? Or are you relying on your loved ones' faith or your own good deeds to secure your standing before God?**

_____

_____

14. ✳ **If you would like to personally accept Jesus' sacrifice for you for the first time, please turn to the last page of this book. Record your reflections.** _____

_____

_____

_____

_____

_____

Day Four

A Match Made in Heaven

It may be surprising to learn that a traditional Jewish wedding ceremony includes part of the *Yom Kippur* confession. Why would such a joyful occasion be punctuated by such a sobering reminder of sin? Perhaps to remind bride and groom that they are not perfect, and should not expect perfection from their lifemate. To remind them that, instead, they must turn to the One who can redeem them from their imperfections and bind them together through His grace and His perfect abiding love.

But there is another, historical, connection. According to the Talmud,[67] the Day of Atonement was a debutante of sorts. Young maidens dressed in white would emerge after the Temple ritual, dancing in the vineyards, calling upon Jerusalem's young men to choose a bride of faith. Even to this day, many orthodox marriages are arranged on *Yom Kippur.*[68]

> Charm is deceptive, and beauty is fleeting; but a woman who fears the Lord is to be praised.
> Proverbs 31:30

With our deeper understanding of the Day of Atonement, and the way in which it was fulfilled by the Messiah at Calvary, this engagement ritual takes on such great meaning for each and every one of us.

1. **Read Isaiah 54:5 and consider your own relationship to God through this lens of betrothal and marriage.** _____

   _____

   _____

   _____

2. **Read Psalm 51:7, Isaiah 1:18, and Revelation 7:14. Reflect on the fact that the young maidens dressed in white garments.[69]**

   _____

   _____

   _____

   _____

3. **Read Isaiah 61:10, and consider that these white courtship garments were to be borrowed, so as not to shame those who had nothing acceptable to wear.[70]** _____

   _____

   _____

   _____

4. **Read John 3:5 and Galatians 3:27. Relate these verses to the fact that these borrowed garments required cleansing by immersion before seeking a betrothal.[71]** _____

   _____

   _____

5. **✳ This biblical betrothal rite took place once the atonement sacrifice was complete.[72] Read Hosea 2:16,19-20 and relate this to your personal relationship with Jesus.** _____

   _____

   _____

   _____

6. ✳ **Imagine or recall the joyful anticipation of those moments when you will gaze/gazed at your bride- or groom-to-be at the start of your wedding ceremony, the gap between you closing with each step down the aisle. Read these verses and share your reaction to God's view of you: Isaiah 62:5b, Ephesians 5:27, and Revelation 19:6-9.** _____

_____

_____

Upon being redeemed from their sin, the sons and daughters of

Jerusalem sought out their brides and grooms. Now, astoundingly, we

find that the very One who redeemed us has chosen us as His soul mate!

The thought literally takes my breath away. How could the perfect,

sinless Son of God choose me, sinner that I am, as His bride? I cannot

imagine being brought home to meet my betrothed's Father, for I am

clearly unworthy of His Son. How could the Father ever approve of

such a union?

Praise the Heavenly Father that

when He looks upon me, He will behold

a radiant bride, as I reflect only the

> The angel said to those who were standing before him, "Take off his filthy clothes...See, I have taken away your sin, and I will put rich garments on you."
>
> Zechariah 3:4

brilliance of my betrothed (see Revelation 21:9-11). Praise God that He

will see nothing but a life of purity, as Christ's righteousness cloaks my

scarlet rags. And praise the Lord that – just like the maidens on *Yom*

Kippur – I won't have to provide my own gown, because I could never afford a gown breathtaking enough for the One who sits on the Throne

of Heaven. Truly, the only acceptable garments for this wedding are the

ones offered by the Bridegroom Himself. Ones cleansed by the blood of

His death and the power of His resurrection.

The One who carried the ugliness of your sin as He died now

> For our light and momentary troubles are achieving for us an eternal glory that far outweighs them all. So we fix our eyes not on what is seen, but on what is unseen. For what is seen is temporary, but what is unseen is eternal.
>
> 2 Corinthians 4:17-18

gazes upon you with anticipation at the person you are becoming. With each day we grow closer to our union with our Savior. The hassles and headaches of engagement are simply drawing us closer to Jesus. And so we fix our eyes on the end of the aisle,

where all of heaven will rejoice over the long-awaited marriage between

the Prince of Peace and the one He cherishes.

7. ✳ **Recall the passage below. What a Suitor! What a celebration! Will you accept His proposal and become His for eternity? Or will you choose to remain alone? Jesus longs to take your hand and draw you into His Father's kingdom forever. Please won't you join Him...?**

> Then I heard what sounded like a great multitude, like the roar of rushing waters and like loud peals of thunder, shouting: "Hallelujah! For our Lord God Almighty reigns. Let us rejoice and be glad and give Him glory! For the wedding of the Lamb has come, and His bride has made herself ready. Fine linen, bright and clean, was given her to wear."
>
> Revelation 19:6-8

Day Five

The Book of Life

The final *Yom Kippur* worship service is called *Neilah*, or locking,

and is still observed by Jews today. The name refers to the impending

locking of heaven's gates to our pleas for

forgiveness, and to the closing of God's Books of

Life and Death. The *Neilah* is punctuated by

confession—confession both of personal sin and

> "Now make confession to the Lord, the God of your fathers, and do His will."
> Ezra 10:11

of God's sovereignty and grace. It is only appropriate, then, to conclude

our study together with confession. A confession of who we are and

who He is, in light of what we have gleaned through this study of His

Law of Atonement.

1. ✳ **Recall the four Hebrew words for sin found in Leviticus 16
   (*tumah*—morally or ceremonially foul; *pesha*—rebellion against
   God; *avon*—the sum of past misdeeds and their deserved
   consequences; and *chatta'ah*—falling short of the perfection of
   God). Read Proverbs 20:9 and Romans 3:23. Confess your sin
   to the One who can and does redeem you from it.** _____
   _____
   _____
   _____
   _____

2. ✳ **Recall the prophetic tabernacle God designed in the
   wilderness. In particular, meditate on the layers of separation**

God instituted between His Holy Self and His sinful children, contrasted with the countless images portrayed in the Tabernacle of the Christ that would one day abolish those dividing walls. Read Ephesians 3:12 and confess your thoughts to the Lord. _____

_____

_____

_____

3. ✳ Recall the physical and ritual purity and the majestic symbolism of the earthly High Priest. Consider your need for an advocate before the Almighty and read these verses about our Great High Priest: Romans 8:34, Hebrews 8:1-2, and Hebrews 9:12. Confess your thoughts to God. _____

_____

_____

_____

4. ✳ Reflect on the perfect blood that God commanded the Israelites to sacrifice before Him in that Most Holy Place. Read Hebrews 9:14 and confess to the Lord your thoughts on how the Cross was your personal Day of Atonement. _____

_____

_____

_____

5. ✳ Read Leviticus 16:29 and recall how the Israelites' life reflected their personal faith in the blood shed for them on that Day of Atonement. Read Romans 10:8-9. Have you accepted Jesus' sacrifice on your behalf? If so, how does your life reflect your individual faith? _____

_____

_____

6. ✳ If you haven't previously accepted Jesus' sacrifice for yourself, would you like to now? If so, please turn to the last page of this book. If not, confess your doubts to God and ask Him to meet you where you are. _____

_____

_____

Yom Kippur is rich. Rich with importance. Rich with prophecy. Rich with salvation. The amazing thing is that each of the separate "components" of the Day of Atonement—God, His Tabernacle, the High Priest, the Sacrifice, and mankind—converged in one Person at the Cross of Calvary.

"In every high and stormy gale, my anchor holds within the veil." These are words from *The Solid Rock*, the classic hymn written by Edward Mote. They speak perfectly to what we have discovered about our Messiah, our Christ, through this study. Our Eternal Anchor holds within the veil, the very residence of God Almighty. Incredibly, that once forbidden place is now is open to anyone who chooses to enter through the Blood of the perfect, final Sacrifice. And instead of an earthly High Priest annually ministering there on our behalf, we now have an immortal High Priest who intercedes for each one of us at every moment of our lives at the very right hand of God.

I pray that as you have explored the Scriptures for yourself these eight weeks, you have personally witnessed the intersection of the Old and the New. That the Torah's law of blood atonement meets its perfect fulfillment through the Blood of Christ. That Jesus did not abolish the

> "Do not think that I have come to abolish the Law or the Prophets; I have not come to abolish them but to fulfill them."
> Matthew 5:17

Jewish faith, but He confirmed it and fulfilled it as no one other than God's Anointed Son could.

We have shared many words about ourselves this Atonement Day…The very act of confronting failings has enabled us to…leave with each other this day…the knowledge that no matter what we do we are the child of God, a valued and irreplaceable jewel in the crown that is God's universe.[73]

From the "Days of Awe" prayer book for the Jewish High Holy Days

Dear friend, that is exactly what you are: an irreplaceable jewel in God's crown! That is why He sent His only Son as *your* Messiah, *your* Christ, *your* Savior. Rejoice in that identity, and shine as the unique, brilliant jewel God created you to be.

I pray that you will, and bid you farewell in the Jewish tradition of the Days of Awe:

> "Rejoice that your names are written in heaven."
> Luke 10:20

May you be inscribed in the Book of Life!

Appendix A

Major Jewish Feasts & Holy Days

There are seven significant feasts or holy days identified in the Jewish Old Testament Scriptures. All are specifically commanded by God, except for Hanukkah and Purim. Further, the Lord demanded pilgrimage to Jerusalem for the Feasts of Passover, Weeks and Tabernacles (see Deuteronomy 16:16; marked with a star in the diagram, right). The chart to the right illustrates where the days fall during the year.

Passover & The Feast of Unleavened Bread *(March/April)*

The Lord commanded the Israelites to observe Passover each year so that they would always remember how He delivered them from slavery in Egypt. On that fateful night, God instructed the Israelites to sacrifice lambs and pain their doorframes with blood, so that the Angel of Death would pass over their households. The next day, as the people fled from Egypt, they did not have time to let their bread dough rise, so they made it without yeast. For that reason, the Lord commanded that the seven-day observance of the Feast of Unleavened Bread be void of any leavening; this is why Jews clear their homes of all food containing yeast before Passover, and eat *matzah* (sheets of unleavened bread) throughout the week. Centuries after this deliverance from bondage in Egypt, Jesus – the Lamb of God who was without sin (leaven) – was sacrificed on Passover to free us from the bondage of our sin.

The Feast of Weeks (Shavuot or Pentecost) *(May/June)*

God commanded the Israelites to bring Him the firstfruits of their crops at the conclusion of the wheat harvest. *Shavuot* (literally "weeks") falls seven weeks (or the fiftieth day) after the second day of Passover (hence the name *Pentecost*, which means "fiftieth" in Greek). Significantly, *Shavuot* also marks the anniversary of when God gave the Law to Moses. It was during this feast that God sent the anointing of the Holy Spirit, fulfilling His promise to write His Word in our hearts (Jeremiah 31:33).

The Feast of Trumpets (Yom Teruah or Rosh Hashanah) *(Sept/Oct)*

During observance of the Feast of Trumpets, a ram's horn, or *shofar*, is blown 100 times, heralding the arrival of the season of repentance. The ten days between the Feast of Trumpets and the Day of Atonement are known as *t'shuva* (literally "turning"), during which Jews personally ask each other for forgiveness of the past year's sins. Now referred to as the Jewish New Year, *Rosh* ("head") *Hashanah* ("of the year") is actually the first day of the *seventh* biblical month; the modern name recognizes a shift in the calendar made during the Babylonian captivity. To usher in a sweet year, *Rosh Hashanah* is celebrated by eating applies and round *challah* bread dipped in honey.

The Day of Atonement (Yom Kippur) *(September/October)*

On this holiest day of the year, the High Priest took the blood of a perfect lamb into the Holy of Holies, where the Lord promised His *shekinah* glory would dwell. There, on the horns of the Mercy Seat, the High Priest offered atonement for the nation with the lamb's blood. Even though the Jerusalem Temple and its altar are no longer standing, Jews still observe Yom Kippur (literally the "Day of Atonement") with a 24-hour fast and a full day of worship and prayers of repentance. On the Cross, our Great High Priest atoned for the sins of all mankind with His own perfect, divine Blood.

The Feast of Tabernacles (Sukkot) *(September/October)*

For seven days, Jews are to live in makeshift *sukkot* ("booths") made with branches and decorated with fruits and vegetables of the season. The roof must be open enough to see the stars and let some rain through. People are to live or eat meals in the tabernacles for the seven-day feast, remembering that their forefathers were sojourners in the wilderness after their deliverance from Egypt. *Sukkot*, a feast similar in feel to American Thanksgiving, is also known as the Feast of (agricultural) Ingathering, or simply, The Feast.

The Feast of Dedication (Hanukkah) *(November/December)*

During the second century before Christ's birth, the Syrians occupied Israel, and their King Antiochus desecrated the Lord's Temple. A grassroots rebellion led by a band of brothers nicknamed the Maccabees ("hammers") defeated the Syrians. The victors cleansed and rededicated the Temple. While there was only enough oil to keep the Lampstand in the Holy Place lit for one day, the Lord miraculously allowed it to last for eight days until a new supply of pressed oil could be delivered. The feast is therefore observed by lighting candles for eight nights. While the instructions for Hanukkah ("dedication") are not found in the Protestant scriptures, we know from John 10:22 that it was observed in Jesus' day.

The Feast of Purim *(February/March)*

This feast celebrates the deliverance of God's people from Haman, the advisor to King Xerces (or Ahasuerus) by Queen Eshter and her uncle Mordechai. *Purim* means "lots" and refers to when Haman cast lots to decide when he would execute the Jews of Persia. The feast is celebrated with a reading of the book of Esther, while the costumed congregation drowns out Haman's name with noisemakers. A favorite treat is *hamantashen* ("Hamen hats"): fruit-filled cookies shaped like the villain's triangular hat.

Appendix B

Garments of the High Priest

Illustration from the Brockhaus and Efron
Jewish Encyclopedia, St. Petersburg, 1906-1913 (public domain)

Appendix C

Yom Kippur Today

The Day of Atonement remains the holiest day on the Jewish
calendar. The faithful fast from food and work, spending the eve and
day of *Yom Kippur* worshipping together in the synagogue. With one
voice, congregations chant the *Al Cheyt*, the Great Confession, pounding
their chests with each recounting of their sins against God, pleading for
His mercy. As worshippers chant praise and petitions to *Avenu Malkeinu*
(Our Father, Our King), the spirit of repentance is palpable.

Yet while the repentance is there, something vital is missing:
atoning blood. You see, the Romans destroyed Jerusalem in 70 A.D.
There was no longer a Temple. No longer a veil. No longer a Holy of
Holies. Rabbis were left with the grim task of deciding how to continue
religious life without God's glorious dwelling and without His sacrificial
altar. Ultimately, the *Yom Kippur* sacrifice of blood became, instead, a
sacrifice of *t'shuva* (returning back to God in repentance), *tefillah* (prayer),
and *tzedakah* (charity). Together, these new sacrifices make up the
modern atonement ritual, observed through five distinct worship services
spanning the twenty-four hours of *Yom Kippur*.

The *Kol Nidre* (All Vows) service begins at sundown.[m] The *Kol Nidre* itself is chanted in Aramaic three times with increasing volume. Through this piece of liturgy, Jews release themselves and others from vows made to God during the previous year. In so doing, worshippers acknowledge their human inability to live up to their promises and provide an opportunity to start off the new year with a clean slate.

The next morning, Jewish families return to the synagogue, stomachs rumbling, for four services that span the entire day. These services include a recounting of the High Priest's journey within the veil of the Holy of Holies during the biblical atonement ritual. The rabbi also teaches from the book of Jonah, expounding on issues related to repentance. *Yom Kippur* worship includes one of four annual *yizkor*, or memorial, services. The *yizkor* provides public acknowledgement of loved ones who have passed away. Throughout the entire day, worship is punctuated by confessions of sin—both personal and corporate.

The Day of Atonement ends with the dramatic *Ne'ilah* (locking) service. Some congregations stand throughout the entire *Ne'ilah*, as they together implore the Lord to forgive them and seal their names in His

---

[m] Jewish holidays always begin at sundown. This is because the creation account is marked by the words, "And there was evening, and there was morning—the first (second, third, etc.) day;" Judaism therefore observes evening as the beginning of each day.

Book of Life before the Gates of Heaven are locked for another year. The service concludes with one long blast of the *shofar*, which is met by the congregation with sighs of relief and joy (and calls for dinner!).

For a faithful Jew, *Yom Kippur* is as beautiful as it is somber: It is an intimate experience between a humble heart and the Almighty God, all the while united with the local and global community of faith. For those with true faith, *Yom Kippur* can evoke overwhelming awe at God's holiness and His abiding love in spite of our sinfulness.

And yet, as worshipful and reverent as the Day of Atonement observance can be, this modern approach is problematic because it leaves out the *atonement*. Nothing is covering us but ourselves and our works, which is no cover at all before Almighty God. The Lord set the

> ...all our righteous acts are like filthy rags.
>
> Isaiah 64:6

price to atone for humanity's sin long ago (Leviticus 17:11) and He never exchanged it for another currency. The only acceptable payment remains perfect blood. After all, there was no Jerusalem Temple when the Day of Atonement commands were given. There was just a portable Tabernacle, one that moved with the Israelites through the desert and the Promised Land for 500 years. So the destruction of the Temple a millennium later did not negate God's demand for a blood substitute. Instead, its destruction signaled that the blood requirement had been forever satisfied. The Messiah's blood paid the price in full for all time. That is why the Lord had no need to reestablish the Temple ever again.

Because blood is absent from today's observance of *Yom Kippur*, many modern Jews have lost touch with our holy God's contempt for sin and His demand for blood to pay for it. This disconnect makes the

> ...I have given you the blood so you can make atonement for your sins. It is the blood, representing life, that brings you atonement.
>
> Leviticus 17:11 NLT

Cross appear to have nothing to do with Judaism, when, in fact, biblical Judaism is drenched in sacrificial, substitutionary blood. By reconnecting with God's demand for blood atonement given in the Torah, perhaps Jews can begin to see how the Torah and the Cross fit logically and beautifully together.

Nevertheless, the Day of Atonement remains the holiest day of the Jewish year. Even nominal Jews fast and drop everything to join with their brethren in synagogues around the globe to confess and repent. They are reminded on that fateful day that *Adonai's* books of Life and Death are shut, and that their names are written in one or the other.

Appendix D

Pronunciation Helps✡

Adam (red)..ah-*dahm*

Al Cheyt (the Great Confession liturgy on Yom Kippur) ....ahl 'hate

Anah (afflict self, fast).. ah-*nah*

Aveenu Malkeinu (Our Father Our King) ..... ah-*vee*-noo mahl-*kay*-noo

Avon (iniquity, punishment for sin) ....aw-*vone*

Azal (to go away) ....aw-*zal*

Azazel (scapegoat) .... az-aw-*zale*

Chata [sin (root)]..'hah-*tah*

Chatta'ah (sin) .... 'hah-tah-*ah*

Chattat (sin offering)... 'hah-*taht*

Chazah (behold, perceive, receive visions) .... 'hah-*zah*

Cohen (priest) .... koh-hane

Dam (blood)..dahm

Ephod (high priest's shoulderpiece)..ay-*fode*

Ez (goat) .... aze

✡ There is no "ch" blend sound in Hebrew as there is in English (e.g., church, chosen). Accordingly, when you see a "ch" in the English transliteration of Hebrew words, it represents a guttural "h" sound (technically a voiceless pharyngeal fricative), much like clearing one's throat. The sound is represented in this pronunciation guide as *'h*. Many English-speakers choose to pronounce the "ch" at the beginning of a word as an "h" sound (e.g. Chanukkah/Hanukkah) or as a "k" sound when it occurs the middle or end of a word (such as *lechem*).

Gat Shemanim (Gethsemane) .... gaht shem-ah-*neem*

Hanukkah (or Chanukkah, Festival of Lights) .... 'hahn-u-*kah*

Kadosh (holy) .... kah-*doesh*

Kaphar (cover, cancel, make atonement) .... kah-*far*

Kapporeth (mercy seat) .... kah-*poor*-et

Kippur (atonement) .... kip-*poor*

Kiyowr (basin) .... kee-*yore*

Kol Nidre (All Vows, Yom Kippur service) .... kole nee-dray

Lechem (bread) .... leh-'*hem*

Meil (high priest's robe of the ephod) .... meh-*eel*

Menorah (candelabra) .... meh-no-*rah*

Minchah (grain offering) .... meen-'*hah*

Neilah (locking, final service of *Yom Kippur*) .... nee-*lah*

Nisan (first month of biblical calendar) .... nee-*sahn*

Olah (burnt offering) .... oh-*lah*

Paniym (Shewbread) .... paw-*neem*

Pentateuch (Five books of Moses, Torah) .... Pen-tah-*tuke*

Pasha (to rebel, revolt, transgress) .... pah-*shah*

Pesha (rebellion) .... peh-*shah*

Rosh Hashanah (Feast of Trumpets) .... *roesh* hah-shah-*nah*

Saba (satisfy or fill) .... sah-*bah*

Sanhedrin (Jewish ruling council until 4th century) .... san-*hee*-drin

Shaba (oath) .... shah-*bah*

Sheba (seven) .... sheh-*bah*

Shabbat (Sabbath) .... shah-*baht*

Shabbaton (great solemn Sabbath) .... shah-bah-*tone*

Shofar (ram's horn) .... show-*fahr*

Sukkot (Feast of Tabernacles) .... soo-*kote*

Tamei (to be foul, unclean) .... tah-*may*

Tamiym (perfect, blameless) .... tah-*meem*

Tefillah (prayer) .... teh-fee-lah

Tehashim (animal skin covering Tabernacle) .... teh-hah-*sheem*

Teruah (trumpets) .... teh-*roo-ah*

Tishri (tenth month of biblical calendar) .... tish-*ree*

Torah (Five Books of Moses) .... toe-*rah*
    (*many American Jews place equal emphasis each syllable*)

T'shuva (repentance, literally "returning") .... t'shoo-*vah*

Tumah (religious impurity) .... toom-*ah*

Tzedakah (charity) .... tseh-dah-kah

Vayikra (name for Leviticus) .... vah-yeek-*rah*

Yizkor (memorial service) .... yiz-core

Yom (day) .... *Yom*e

Yom Kippur (Day of Atonement) .... *Yom*e kip-*poor*

Appendix E
Bibliography

Acacia (1980). In Academic American Encyclopedia (Vol. 1). Arête Publishing Company: Princeton, NJ.

American Academy of Religion (1995). The HarperCollins Dictionary of Religion. San Francisco: HarperCollins Publishers, Inc.

Baron, D. (1888). Rays of Messiah's Glory: Christ in the Old Testament. Alpha Publications: Winona Lake, IN.

Bloch, A. P. (1978). The Biblical and Historical Background of the Jewish Holy Days. Ktav Publishing House, Inc.: New York.

Brown, F., Driver, S, Briggs, C. (1996). Brown-Driver-Briggs Hebrew and English Lexicon. Hendrickson Publishers: Peabody, MA.

Carson, D. A. (1984). In The Expositor's Bible Commentary, Volume 8, Frank E. Gaebelein, ed., pp. 3-601. Zondervan Bible Publishers: Grand Rapids.

Chambers, O. (1935). My Utmost for His Highest. Barbour and Company, Inc.: Westwood, NJ.

Church, L. F. (1961). Matthew Henry's Commentary: In One Volume. Zondervan: Grand Rapids, MI.

Cohen, J. M. (1997). 1,001 Questions and Answers on *Rosh Hashanah* and *Yom Kippur*. Jason Aronson, Inc.: Northvale, NJ.

Edersheim, A. (1994). The Temple: Its Ministry and Services (Updated Edition). Hendricson Publishers, Inc.: Peabody, MA.

Fox, E. (1995). The Five Books of Moses: Genesis, Exodus, Leviticus, Numbers, Deuteronomy: A New Translation with Introductions, Commentary, and Notes. Schocken Books, Inc.: New York.

Frankel, E. (1996). The Five Books of Miriam: A Woman's
Commentary on the Torah. G. P. Putnam's Sons: New York.

"Gethsemane." Encyclopaedia Britannica [On-line]. 2004.
Encyclopaedia Britannica Premium Service.
<http//www.britannica.com>. Accessed December 9, 2004.

Glatzer, N. N. (1968). On the Bible: Eighteen Studies by Martin Buber.
Schocken Books: New York.

Greetham, P. (1996). King Herod the Great. In The Nativity Pages
[On-line].
<http://ourworld.compuserve.com/homepages/p_greetham/wi
semen/wmsoc9.html>.

Grieve, M. (1995). Frankincense. In Botanical.com: A Modern Herbal
[On-line].
<http://www.botanical.com/botanical/mgmh/f/franki31.html>.
Accessed November 6, 2002.

Rosenfeld, A. (2004). Halacha Overview. In Project Genesis, Inc.
[Online]. <http://www.torah.org>. Accessed December 20,
2004.

Hall, D. M. (2004). Ceremonial Immersion in Mikveh. In Zion Messianic
Fellowship [Online]. <http://www.tzion.org>. Accessed
December 20, 2004.

Halley, H. H. (1965). Halley's Bible Handbook. Zondervan Publishing
House: Grand Rapids, MI.

Hanson, K. (1997). Dead Sea Scrolls: The Untold Story. Council Oak
Books: Tulsa, OK.

Hirsch, E. G. (2002). High Priest. In Jewish Encyclopedia [On-line].
<http://www.jewishencyclopedia.com>. Accessed December
11, 2003.

Holy Materials, The (1998). In The Bible Knowledge Accelerator [On-
line]. <http://www.bible-

history.com/tabernacle/TAB4Preparing_for_the_Tabernacle.ht
m>. Accessed October 4, 2002.

Kaiser, W. C. Jr. (1990). Exodus. In The Expositor's Bible
Commentary, Volume 2, Frank E. Gaebelein, ed., pp. 285-497.
Zondervan Bible Publishers: Grand Rapids.

Levine, B. A. (1989). The JPS Torah Commentary: Leviticus. The
Jewish Publication Society: New York.

Levy, R. N. (1985). On Wings of Awe: A Machzor for Rosh Hashanah
and Yom Kippur. B'nai B'rith Hillel Foundations: Washington,
D.C.

Little, D. (1989). The Tabernacle in the Wilderness (2nd ed.). Loizeaux
Brothers: Neptune, NJ.

Meier, P. D. (1993). The Third Millennium. Thomas Nelson
Publishing: Nashville, TN.

Murray, J. (1955). Redemption: Accomplished and Applied. William B.
Eerdmans Publishing Company: Grand Rapids, MI.

Punton, A. (2002). The World Jesus Knew. Moody Press: Chicago.

Rich, T. R. (1996). Human Nature. In Judaism 101 [Online].
<http://www.jewfaq.org/human.htm>. Accessed March 31,
2002.

Robinson, G. (2000). Essential Judaism: A Complete Guide to Beliefs,
Customs and Rituals. Pocket Books/Simon & Schuster, Inc.:
New York.

Rosenberg, S. E. (1961). Bridge to Brotherhood: Judaism's Dialogue
with Christianity. Abelard-Schuman: New York.

Schaetz, T. C. (2002). Begging for Myrrh. Christian Parenting Today,
Volume 15(2):30, Winter 2002.

Steinsaltz, A. (1976). The Essential Talmud. Basic Books, Inc.: New
York.

Stern, D. H. (1992). Jewish New Testament Commentary. Jewish New Testament Publications: Clarksville, MD.

Taylor, P. S., (2002). Did the High Priest Enter the Holy of Holies With Rope Around His Ankle? [On-line]. Available <http://www.christiananswers.net>. Accessed August 12, 2002.

Thompson, F. C. (1983). The Thompson Chain-Reference Bible, New International Version. B. B. Kirkbride Bible Co., Inc.: Indianapolis, and The Zondervan Corporation: Grand Rapids, MI.

Tierney, J. J. (2003). High Priest. In Catholic Encyclopedia, Volume XII. [Online]. <http://www.newadvent.org>. Accessed December 11, 2003.

Trepp, L. (1980). The Complete Book of Jewish Observance. Behrman House, Inc./Summit Books: New York.

Yaseen, L. C. (1985). The Jesus Connection to Triumph Over Anti-Semitism. Crossroad: New York.

Zodhiates, S. (1990). The Hebrew-Greek Key Study Bible (New American Standard, Red Letter Edition). AMG Publishers: Chattanooga, TN.

Zion Messianic Jewish Fellowship Congregation (Austin, Texas). Online. Available <http://tzion.org/articles/Temple1.html>. Accessed August 12, 2002.

Notes

1 Exodus 3:8,17 (among numerous others)
2 Exodus 16:31
3 Matthew 5:17
4 Fox, E. (1995)
5 Zodhiates, S. (1990)
6 Zodhiates, S. (1990)
7 Zodhiates, S. (1990)
8 Bloch, A. P. (1978), and Trepp, L. (1980)
9 Fox, E. (1995)
10 Edersheim, A. (1994)
11 Zodhiates, S. (1990)
12 Brown, F., Driver, S, and Briggs, C. (1996)
13 Leviticus 16:29,31 and 23:32
14 Zodhiates, S. (1990)
15 Fox, E. (1995)
16 Little, D. (1989)
17 Little, D. (1989)
18 Acacia (1980)
19 Little, D. (1989), Acacia (1980)
20 Zion Messianic Jewish Fellowship Congregation (2002)
21 Little, D. (1989), Holy Materials (1998), Victorie, Inc. (2005)
22 Victorie, Inc. (2005)
23 Little, D. (1989), Holy Materials (1998), Victorie, Inc. (2005)
24 Holy Materials (1998), Victorie, Inc. (2005)
25 Grieve, M. (1995), Schaetz, T. (2002)
26 Schaetz, T. (2002)
27 Little, D. (1989), Holy Materials (1998), Victorie, Inc. (2005)
28 Grieve, M. (1995)
29 Edersheim, A. (1994)
30 Edersheim, A. (1994)
31 Church, L. F. (1961)
32 Kaiser, W. (1990)
33 Little, D. (1989), Church, L. F. (1961)
34 Luke 22:44
35 Little, D. (1989)
36 John 12:36
37 Holy Materials (1998)
38 Edersheim, A. (1995)
39 Exodus 30:20
40 Hebrews 4:14
41 Numbers 3:11-12; 8:16,18; Trepp, L. (1980)
42 Frankel, E. (1996)
43 Punton, A. (1996)
44 Edersheim, A. (1994)
45 Edersheim, A. (1994)
46 Edersheim, A. (1994)
47 Bloch, A. P. (1978)

[48] Carson, D. A. (1984)
[49] Thompson, F. C. (1983); Edersheim, A. (1994)
[50] Punton, A. (1996)
[51] Exodus 12:13
[52] Church, L. F. (1961)
[53] Chambers, O. (1935)
[54] Zodhiates, S. (1990)
[55] Halley, H. (1965)
[56] Zodhiates, S. (1990)
[57] Edersheim, A. (1994)
[58] Levine, B. A. (1989)
[59] Levine, B. A. (1989)
[60] Levine, B. A. (1989)
[61] Edersheim, A. (1994), Fox, E. (1995)
[62] Bloch, A. (1978)
[63] Bloch, A. (1978), Edersheim, A. (1994)
[64] Edersheim, A. (1994)
[65] Thompson, F. C. (1983)
[66] Edersheim, A. (1994), Punton, A. (2002)
[67] Mishnah Taanit 4:8
[68] Cohen, J. M. (1997)
[69] Cohen, J. M. (1997)
[70] Cohen, J. M. (1997)
[71] Cohen, J. M. (1997)
[72] Cohen, J. M. (1997)
[73] Levy, R. N. (1985)

About the Author

Tammy Priest grew up in a Jewish family where she learned the traditions of her faith. She embraced her heritage and became active in her local synagogue, continuing her involvement as a university student. Then one morning as she sang, God audibly spoke to the college senior with words she had never heard before: "Jesus is the Messiah."

Since that day, Tammy has been sharing the powerful testimony of her conversion. She also enjoys teaching adults and children about the ways in which God's Old Testament and its rituals pointed perfectly to the coming Christ.

Tammy resides in Winston-Salem, North Carolina, with her husband, David, and their two children.

To learn more about Tammy's ministry, please visit her website www.beginningwithmoses.com.

God created you so that He could have a personal relationship with you—both here on earth and in heaven for eternity. Without that relationship, life often feels like a never-ending quest for answers and meaning. But with it, everything in life takes on perspective and purpose. Do you desire to have that kind of relationship? To have such a personal relationship with the God of Creation that you can personally experience His goodness, strength, and peace each day?

If so, it is as simple as observing the Day of Atonement:

1. Acknowledge that you are a sinner—someone who has done wrong things, thought bad thoughts, rebelled against God, or who simply falls short of God's holy perfection.

2. Accept that God's Son, Jesus the Messiah, shed His blood to pay the Old Testament price for your sin once and for all, and that He conquered the grave so that you, too, may live beyond this life (Romans 10:9).

Pray to receive His gift of atonement for you today:

God, I confess to you that I am sinful—a person who has done wrong and who falls short of divine perfection. I desire to be cleansed and forgiven of that sin so that I might know You and experience true life on earth and one day in heaven. I accept the sacrifice of your Son as the price for my forgiveness. Please come to live within me. Teach me about who You are, and who I truly am and can become. Amen.

If you prayed this prayer—or one like it—with sincerity, then your name has been sealed in God's Book of Life! Pray to Him, study His Scriptures, and fellowship with other believers, so that you can grow in your faith and understanding of who God is, and who you are in Him.

Made in the USA
Coppell, TX
19 January 2022